I Should Have Honor

I Should Have Honor

A MEMOIR OF HOPE AND
PRIDE IN PAKISTAN

KHALIDA BROHI

RANDOM HOUSE

NEW YORK

In loving memory of my late mother-in-law, Mary Ellen. You were a strong woman and loving mother. You looked me in the eye and asked me who I am. You entrusted me with your only son and made our life together possible. You were a truly honorable woman and your memory will always be a blessing to us and so many others. I love you, Mom. We miss you.

Contents

PART TWO

Introduction

THERE IS A SAYING IN MY TRIBE: *IZZAT MARE, PEN MARE te maf.*

"Even if I have nothing, I should have honor."

Like any other girl in my village, I associated the concepts of honor and dishonor with my father. I knew, in the way that I knew the sun rises from the east, that as his eldest daughter, I was the person who could dishonor him the most. In my childhood I would spend days and hours worrying about how to keep the honor of my father alive, and how never to stain it.

Every time I thought of honor, a small girl would come to mind, a girl wearing a long chador (veil), standing behind the weatherbeaten wooden door of her house, peeking through the cracks, staring at me while I played with my friends in the streets. She would be one of the girls in the village who wasn't allowed to play with me and my friends as we ran around yelling at one another, playing *kho* (hide-and-seek) or making clay dolls. She was each of those girls who stayed behind, peeking from the windows and doors when I went to call them to play. There were moments in our game of *kho* when I would steal a glimpse of these girls and feel a stab of jealousy in my heart for how strong they must be, to stay behind at home and honor their fathers. I wished I could do that. Or I wished I were forced to do that. But instead games, clay dolls, and experiences running free were my reality.

At times I would see my cousins run off, their faces flushed, hiding smiles, the corner of their scarves stuffed in their mouths each time their mothers spoke about their marriages. "Look at the honor of my house," the mother would beam, "shy as a little kitten!" The jealousy would return. . . . *I would never feel so shy perhaps. I am definitely going to dishonor my father,* I would think to myself with a sinking heart.

As I grew older, my innocent understanding of honor and dishonor expanded through hushed whispers of the women in our *haveli* (traditional communal home of an extended family). As the word *murder* emerged in the same conversations as *honor,* my fear and anxiety about this topic became stronger—women and girls killed because they brought shame on their male relatives and their houses. The biggest dishonor to a house, it seemed, was a girl gone "wrong." Never really understanding what that meant, I had promised myself I would never go "wrong."

Then one day when I was about ten years old, my father sat me down and asked me the question I dreaded the most.

"Khali," he said in a tone that made no effort to hide his

affection and worry, "do you know how you will dishonor me?" Blood drained from my round cheeks, my mouth became dry, and I felt light-headed and heavy in my body at the same time. I didn't say anything, understanding very well that he knew the answer to his question. He knew clearly but wanted to hear it from me.

I did not want to say it aloud. The idea of going "wrong" was a bitter taste in my mouth, a devil lurking in the woods, a ghost hiding behind doors, all those things I feared. And yet I didn't even know what "wrong" meant. So I kept quiet, letting the thick air hold me still as my breathing turned shallow.

My father's eyes looked straight into mine. Fear now took physical shape and danced in front of my eyes as I stared back at him, afraid that he could see it too.

"Khali," he continued with the same grimness, "you will dishonor me the day you fail to bring good grades home."

I thought I was not hearing him correctly. "I have risked every bit of my dignity by bringing you and your sisters to the city," he continued. "I have brought tears into my own father's eyes. I have argued with my friends about my decision to give you freedom, and with this freedom they tell me you can easily destroy my honor. My honor now lies with you, my Khali, and the day you stop working hard and fail in school, I will be completely dishonored."

He kept speaking, but I wasn't able to hear anything else. My universe was slowly taking a new shape around me. My mind and heart filled with fresh awareness, and my brain opened with the burst of this new knowledge. A secret was spoken to me that day, a secret that would later help me stand strong in the face of a centuries-old custom. Life would later call me to speak this truth. I would be able to remind people what honor *really* meant. Honor is not murder. And dishonor is not a girl who goes to school. It is not a girl who plays outside. It is not a girl who refuses to marry at a young age. It is not a girl who speaks, laughs, and takes the opportunities that come in front of her. Instead, honor is identity. Honor is dignity. Honor is serving those we love with integrity and hard work; it is respecting one another, welcoming the stranger, and speaking and being proud of your own language. It is providing for your family, striving for the best in life, and praying for the best for people; it is being a nation that people praise and respect.

This awakening to the real meaning of honor gave me the clarity to be angry when a murder close to my home shook my understanding of the world. I stood up to fight this unjust crime. And I started on a journey of reminding people what true honor is. I would raise my voice, look deep into our cultural values, and ask, *Where exactly did honor attach itself to murder?* I would examine our religious guidance to try to understand how the Holy Quran could call daughters *rehmat* (blessing) when people who called themselves Muslims were practicing this brutal custom.

That day my father took the biggest weight from my shoulders and in its place attached two wings. I soared in this new awareness. I was free from the fear that makes women tell their peers to accept their fate, to stay quiet in the face of injustice. And more than anything, I was free to tell my story and the stories of those like me to the world.

I wrote this book because it is time to share this story. My story is not unique. It is the story of thousands of girls and women in Pakistan who are unable to grow because of a lack of opportunities or lack of voice.

I proudly call myself a tribal woman, and I carry with me hundreds of stories that have shaped and enriched my life and connected me to every single woman in my country. But it is time to have an intimate conversation about the taboos surrounding honor killings, to share stories and expose the complexities of a society that gets easily overgeneralized, never letting us have a deeper sense of why these issues are still rampant.

I was born in a tribal area of Pakistan, moved among rural communities, slum communities, towns, and cities, and even set foot in elite circles. I came to see firsthand what has made my country strong. Despite honor killings and poverty, people in Pakistan thrive and continue to grow. I want to move the conversation from politics to people, toward real human stories. Because at the end of the day, we are solving real human issues.

Finally, I wrote this book because I truly believe in honor. Honor has been misused for centuries. We have come to feel it is ugly and unnecessary. But in reality it is a beautiful, powerful value that grounds us and makes us stronger. It is time now to redefine honor and make it a part of each and every one of us. Honor is what gives us the strength to fight for what is right, to stand up for justice, for goodness, to be strong in faith and belief, and to defend our bodies, our cultures, and our environment. By reclaiming our honor, we will take the power away from those who use it against us. By taking charge of our identity, we will stop those who decide our fate. And by believing that we should have honor, we will start on the journey to being stronger in ourselves.

I often meet young people who are excited about a cause but are waiting for that one thing that will help them begin. But you already have all you need to start. I take pride that I created paths where no path existed, that I mobilized people and organized groups where it appeared the hardest. My life has constantly brought moments where I had to make one decision: *If the resources to help me with my goal do not exist, do I wait for them to materialize, or do I create them myself?* I realized while writing this book that I was able to create them from nothing because of a deeply rooted sense of justice, of honor. Honor in that sense was my fuel and the source of my innovation, whether it meant using only ten minutes of Internet time to create an online campaign, or bringing tribal men together by organizing a cricket match. Finding what gives you honor will empower you with the determination and creativity you need to create anything you imagine, anything that gives you great joy.

Part One

CHAPTER I

Light of the World

LONG BEFORE I WAS BORN, MY MOTHER LIVED IN A small village in the heart of the vast rugged mountains of Balochistan, Pakistan's largest province. Everywhere you looked, there were dry, tall mountains, dotted with wild shrubs and pink flowers. Many tribes call this land home, including mine, the Brahui, who have been part of it for nearly five thousand years. Balochistan, though mostly dry and barren, is a vast, colorful, and largely unpopulated land with a beautiful coast that boasts one of the greatest natural ports in the world, one coveted by many governments through history. Vast blue sky envelops valleys, villages, and towns. The people are shepherds, farmers, homesteaders, and local entrepreneurs. They cling to their traditions with their hearts and to their honor with pride.

Noor Jehan means "light of the world." True to her name, my mother grew to be an indigenous girl with a big heart and a spirit full of wonder, faith, and immense love for her tribe. She was the third of nine children, and like many children in her village, she became an adult at a very young age. Most children are given only the first two years for infancy, then three years to learn to be responsible. Around the age of seven or eight, children get busy helping their parents with daily chores, taking care of other, younger siblings, and, in the case of boys, sometimes even earning income for the family. Taking on adult responsibilities makes the majority of children *look* like adults. Oftentimes they are betrothed to be married at the first trace of puberty.

For my mother, that transition from childhood to adulthood was not easy. As a free spirit, she found it hard not to run around with the wind. But responsibilities soon started to tie her down. By the age of three, she was helping her mother in the house. By the time she was eight, she was practically managing the home on her own. Every morning when my *bhalla ama* (literally "big mother," grandmother) crossed the small stream that flowed near their mud *haveli* (the traditional family compound) to the vegetable fields to help my grandfather plant new seeds or harvest, it was my mother who swept the kitchen and washed the dishes while squatting on the dirt floor. She dunked a rag into the ashes from the previous night's wood and scrubbed every pot and steel plate until her little arms ached. She rinsed the dishes in a clean bowl of water, then placed them in a metal basket to dry, eventually lining up the clean pots and pans neatly on the wooden shelf that my *bhalla aba* (grandfather) had built from a tree he once chopped. Then she swept the dirt floor with a hand broom made of dried date leaves, crouching to brush the compacted earth as if shooing away a mouse, until the dirt floor lay perfectly smooth and flawless. Finally, after she completed all these chores, she picked up her younger sister Lal Bibi (Diamond), just a toddler at the time, and walked to the fields to meet her mother so she could nurse the baby.

Although Noor Jehan was an obedient child, she was also adventurous and sometimes impatient. Unhappy with her endless chores, she tried to finish them as quickly as possible so she could run off to the trees and find her friends. Sometimes she had to bathe the baby before taking her to nurse with her mother, and if the baby cried too hard, she would secretly pinch her on the arm to make her stop. Life was hard for everyone, and it was never too early to learn that.

Despite the hardships, Noor Jehan had an infectious humor, boundless positivity, and a sense of possibility. She wanted to run. She wanted to do things that made her feel free. While other girls in the village played with dolls and performed weddings with them, my mother climbed up the old pomegranate tree in the yard of the mud *haveli*. When the wind blew dirt and the soft scent of the fresh spring water, she would climb higher and pretend to be on top of the world, the fragrant breeze licking her little face.

She played *fitu* (hopscotch) with her friends, making marks on the ground and jumping in them without touching the lines. As the sun set every night, she sat with her siblings and parents listening to the stories of wild animals that her father or uncle had encountered, wonder filling every part of her, and stars filling the sky over her head.

Then one summer day when my mother was nine years old, everything changed forever.

CHAPTER 2

The Exchange

IT WAS AN EARLY MORNING LIKE ALL THE OTHERS. THE sun peeked slowly over the tip of the mountains, and the sky was its brightest blue with feathery clouds sleepily drifting through. A donkey cart stopped near the *haveli*. Like most donkey carts in Pakistan, this one was a simple platform over two wheels with a harness for one donkey. The driver sat crossed-legged at the reins holding a switch. The cart was old and worn, with the odd wobble, yet was versatile enough to carry any load. It worked hard like everything else. The donkey was in about the same condition. The cart came to an unceremonious stop at the gate, and Mohim Khan, my maternal grandfather, climbed down, beaming with joy.

Bhalla Aba was—and still is—a tall, thin man with a shorn head and a large toothless smile. Lore has it that he used to be very handsome, with great powers of influence and persuasion. Even in poverty he wore pure cotton dresses that were soaked in rice starch to make them stiff, adding to his distinguished, sharp look. "Sharam Naz," he called out to his wife, a hint of decision in his voice. Then he called out to my mother who paused while scooping some water from the bucket where she was washing her siblings before breakfast. "Come now! We're all going to Sindh."

"Sindh! Really?" my mother exclaimed in happy surprise. She and her siblings had heard about Sindh in stories told over chai or at bedtime on the *charpoys*, the woven wooden cots that they dragged from a corner every night to sleep under the naked sky, sandwiched warmly between *rilis* (traditional quilts). Never had they dreamed of going there. She saw the uncles and aunts who lived there only when they came to visit in Balochistan. So going all the way down to that foreign land was the biggest *mistai* (good news) she had ever heard!

My mother excitedly washed the faces of her brothers and sisters, full of joy. She collected the bedrolls that they would spread each night on the *charpoys* (a task her mother usually did), and she collected cow dung and wood to make fire for the breakfast chai. Bhalla Ama and Bhalla Aba spoke in hushed tones in a dark room in a corner of the *haveli*.

My grandfather had paid a visit to his four brothers in the village of Gandakho, in the district of Larkana, Sindh, which borders Balochistan. The same district of the great family of Zulfiqar Ali Bhutto and his daughter Benazir Bhutto, who would both lead the country as popular prime ministers. Bhalla Aba's brothers lived there with their families working as day laborers in the fields of landlords. My grandfather once lived among his brothers, but after the great floods that hit Sindh in 1973, he fled to Balochistan and bought the land where their mud *haveli* stands today. It was a wise decision, because more floods plagued the province after he moved. Many families lost everything, but his brothers refused to give up the lives they had created, believing their chances of earning more income were greater in Sindh than in Balochistan, where the land is more rocky and dry. People in Balochistan live mainly on wage labor, shopkeeping, or herding sheep rather than agriculture.

My grandfather would occasionally get on the bus and make the eleven-hour journey through the mountains on Wangu Road to visit his brothers. This time he had just returned from a trip there, during which he discovered that his youngest brother had fallen in love with a girl he had seen at a wedding. She was also Brahui but a member of the Jattak clan. He and his brothers were members of the Mengal clan. Marriages between different clans were not common, but they were also not impossible. It was, and still is, common for clans that don't mix often to swap girls for marriage. To make up for the lack of trust, a daughter from the groom's clan will be married to a son in the bride's clan. If one clan harmed the bride, the exchange bride would have to face the consequences. About 30 percent of all marriages in Pakistan are these exchange marriages, commonly known as *wata sata*.

My grandfather had accompanied his brothers to go ask for the hand of the girl his youngest brother had seen at the wedding. When they did, her father had demanded a *badli*—an exchange. This was hard as all the brothers were young, with no children or no daughters. Then my grand-father thought of his four daughters, who were still very young. He loved them dearly, but for a brother one must give his life! He put forward the offer of my mother, the eldest of his girls, as the *badli*. My uncle's bride and my mother acted as a kind of collateral for each other. It was a moment of great pride and honor for all the men. The sacrifice that Bhalla Aba was offering was like giving one of his limbs. It made his brothers proud. None of them considered the consequences to the lives that they were trading like livestock, because these lives were their only sources of wealth, their only valuable possessions. To trade them showed not only their power but also their generosity.

So while Bhalla Aba's brother was going to be happily marrying a woman of his choosing, my nine-year-old mother was to be offered to three different men in the Jattak family, starting with the eldest, Liaqat, who was about thirty at that time. Liaqat refused immediately, having heard of my mother's frail thin body, saying she was too ugly. The second son to whom she was offered (age twenty-eight) already had several children who were the same age as my mother. He refused her as well with the same words, adding that he could find a second wife anytime he wanted. And so the decision was made for Noor Jehan to be given to the second-to-last son in the family, Sikander, who at the time was only thirteen and the only one among them striving for an education.

Sikander was different from his brothers. Aside from being the second youngest, he was also the most curious. He somehow knew that there was a much bigger world beyond the walls of his family hut, beyond the village, beyond Pakistan even. And he was inspired to discover it. While all his brothers proudly went to work in the fields with their father, he dreamed of leaving his small world and being educated. He loved to read books and even dreamed of owning a library one day. He awoke every morning at four to walk for hours on the dirt road that led to the village next to his to attend the closest school. When he arrived at the school, the wind had often blown so much dirt on his face that the teachers failed to recognize him and refused to let him in. So he would find a puddle or trough of water and scrub his face, return to the classroom, identify himself—and walk into his world of education, his road out of poverty and into a new life, a world of his own making.

My paternal grandfather, Allah Ditta (God Given), was a stern conservative man with a booming voice and strict values. He nonetheless encouraged Sikander in his quest for education, after seeing how committed he was. And because Sikander had their father's approval, his elder brothers had often bought him a notebook or a pen from their modest wages. They were oddly inspired by their curious little brother. They lacked his drive but were proud to be able to support him. The eldest, Liaqat, took a particular interest in encouraging him, buying him oil paints (which he used to paint a big Pakistani flag on the mud walls of their house) and pictures of prominent politicians as if from some distant land. Liaqat encouraged Sikander to dream of a life in politics, maybe even in Islamabad, an inconceivably distant place for the son of a poor farmer.

But the exchange marriage to my mother challenged all my father's dreams. Getting married as a child was not part of the plan he envisioned for himself: he saw it as a trap to keep him from realizing his potential. On the day his brothers and father came to tell him about his upcoming marriage, he was sitting on the floor of their bamboo shack, studying from his geography textbook.

The shock froze his face. "But Father!" he said. "I have more studies, and so much more to learn!"

His father, though torn, knew he had indulged his son's fantasies long enough. His tradition demanded an exchange, and a bride had to come to this house to keep the honor of this family.

"A bride won't stop you from getting an education!" he replied sternly, and left the room.

And so it was settled. The nine-year-old girl would marry the thirteen-year-old boy.

CHAPTER 3

Bundle of Hope

NOOR JEHAN, BLISSFULLY UNAWARE, CAREFULLY SPREAD her worn yellow scarf with the big red flowers and bright green leaves over the dirt floor. She gleefully took her only dress, the baby's cloth diapers, some baby clothes, and a bag of chips that her second eldest brother (who secretly was her favorite) had sneaked to her from his wage money. She placed all these things in the middle of the scarf, gathered the four corners, and tied them tightly. She tucked the bundle under her arm, happily rejoining the family outside. She was ready for the journey to Sindh.

Meanwhile Bhalla Ama was bathing the infant in a big tin plate that my mother often used to wash clothes. Her foot firmly planted in the plate, she held the baby straddling her ankle with one hand while using the other to scoop warm water over her. Bhalla Ama had not shown any signs of joy at this sudden trip, which surprised Noor Jehan. In fact, her mother was quieter and a little more preoccupied with her thoughts than normal. Everyone knew Bhalla Ama didn't show her joy on the outside. She considered it unladylike to giggle and chortle. Only the occasional warm smile told those who knew her that she was in fact happy. But today Noor Jehan saw no trace of a smile on her mother's face.

My mother knew that Bhalla Ama had been married off at eleven to Bhalla Aba, who was ten years older than she. It is common in my culture for guests in a house to catch a glimpse of the young women, maybe even be served by them. Sometimes those glimpses turn into marriage proposals. Many times families will hide their women before guests arrive to preserve their purity and avoid such proposals. Declining a proposal can cause lasting strife between two families. In the case of my grandmother, she had caught the eye of Bhalla Aba's parents for her grace and maturity. And because she was old enough to have children, her parents agreed to marry her off, receiving a sum of money in exchange. She had lived a life of difficulty, poverty, and diseases. She worked hard and through her wisdom transformed the heart of her husband.

"Sabr," Bhalla Ama would tell my mother years later, *"sabr* [patience] is the true virtue of a woman. If I hadn't had patience, today we would not be living this good life. Do remember that, my daughter," she would repeat over and over. And my mother would promise to remember, because in her heart she knew one thing about Bhalla Ama— she never lied.

Noor Jehan was not given any details about what was happening that fateful day, and it would likely have been difficult to help her understand. She was only nine. Unlike her mother at her wedding, she showed no signs of puberty. Her childhood was cut even shorter than that of her peers. To this day, my mother's eyes fill with sadness at the thought of never having said a proper goodbye to her mud *haveli,* or to that old pomegranate tree and the fabric doll she left behind, or to those friends playing in the corner of the street and giggling as their eyes twinkled in the sunlight.

But in that moment, the excitement of going to a foreign land had overcome any other thoughts in her mind. She sat next to Bhalla Ama on the brightly painted bus, staring out the window in anticipation as the road moved fast beneath her. She enjoyed imagining the stories of the people she saw through the windows. She admired their mud houses and the mountains beyond the ones she had known. When the bus stopped to let passengers on and off, fruit or snack *walas* (vendors) on the side of the road would pass coconut pieces, water, or chips through the windows to eager hands. It was exciting to share sweets with her family and gaze eagerly at the sights sweeping by. As night fell and the road became black, the sound of sweet love songs playing on the radio and the gentle heaving of the road lulled her to sleep.

The next morning, as the sun spread in the sky, breaking the darkness over vast green fields, the trees swung in the wind. Finally the bus arrived at a small open ground, its final station. My mother smiled with sleepy eyes and a happy heart. She had already fallen in love with this new land, with its wind, with the herds of cows churning dirt beneath their hooves. There were no mountains, only flat green fields of rice, okra, wheat, and sunflowers, but they filled her heart with joy.

The family went to the village where my mother was to meet her young husband. She was still oblivious to what was happening. They were greeted at the gate and led inside. As she passed, the women of the *haveli* stared and whispered to one another. As she sat in this strange home taking in the new surroundings, she didn't know that her hosts were judging her. They were disappointed. They had given up a beautiful girl in marriage to an unknown family and received in exchange, they realized, a tiny, skinny girl. My mother, malnourished and chronically anemic, was not much to look at. So my father's family demanded further compensation—not just one but *two* girls—from my mother's family. It was decided that the firstborn girl of my maternal uncle would be married into my father's family. With one word, the elders made the decision. *Phidi*, which means "from the belly," was the ritual, and it was marked on a stone.

In this way—in one brief moment—a gathering of men, a few quiet women, and some religious leaders sealed the fate of three women across two generations. I grew up to know it as a woman's fate. My aunts would say to one another, "It's our fate, my dear one, sob as much as you want. Go in a corner and shed your tears, but you come back to this house, to this reality, and in the end it's you who faces it all. So just accept it."

CHAPTER 4

Dreams of My Father

AMID VAST FIELDS OF GREENS AND YELLOWS, WITH purple flowers, large trees, and small streams running throughout, lay the village of Satanave, where my father grew up. Sindh, with its beauty and ancient culture, has been home to renowned Sufi poets, artists, and lovers. Songs in this land praise the countryside, the sky above it, and the beautiful channel that the vast Indus River carves through the heart of this province. Sindh is a place of color, music, and simple people, the majority living in small shacks made of bamboo, hay, and tree trunks, like my father's. Unlike Balochistan, the land in this part of the country is flat, wet, and suitable for farming, and it is more heavily populated. The provincial capital, Karachi, is the biggest city in Pakistan and also its financial center. But Sikander, born into a family of five brothers and four sisters, was far removed from urban life. The son of a share-cropper, he was the second-to-last brother, and like every boy in his village, he was expected to generate income for his family. While his elder brothers helped their father in the fields growing rice and wheat for rich landlords who paid them a pittance, my father, at the age of four, was assigned to herd goats with his same-age friend Durroo, for his house and for the neighbors'.

Every morning after breakfast, which included a cup of sweet chai and dried *roti* (flatbread baked over an open fire), he went along with Durroo to herd goats in the neighborhood lands. They would walk, sometimes barefoot, sticks in hand, with about a dozen goats ahead of them. Sometimes they sang or hummed a Sindhi song that they had heard on the radio. Sometimes Durroo would talk and my father would daydream, a habit that stayed with him into adulthood. As a child, he could easily walk into a dream in the bright of day. He would think about and analyze everything, from strategies to win at playing marbles, to how the stars hung in the sky, to why his father, Allah Ditta, gave such importance to people from a certain caste.

Sikander, though very young, had an intuitive sense of justice. He had developed a dislike for those given special and unearned treatment. He knew his father was not a very educated man, but to sit, as his father did, at the feet of men and ask for their prayer simply because of their heritage—and they were not necessarily good people—felt very wrong to him. As a young boy, my father was already questioning the culture and traditions he'd been raised in.

While herding goats one quiet day, Sikander hummed and chatted with Durroo. The sun rose high over their heads, marking the afternoon. When they came to a lush green pasture, they stopped the herd, sat down, and opened their meals that his sister had packed that morning: *jaggary* (raw cane sugar) atop freshly made *roti,* tied inside a piece of fabric so that the warm bread melted the sugar into a delicious sticky syrup. As Durroo and my father ate, they gazed up at the big blue sky that enveloped their small familiar world, cherishing the day's stillness. It was hot, but a soothing breeze occasionally made the trees in the distance dance, which my father found delightful.

As the sun set on this ordinary day, Durroo was sleeping next to the river. Sikander came out of his thoughts and noticed that something was wrong with the goats. They were not moving. He took his stick and went to investigate. To his horror, he discovered they were desperately bloated and in distress. It turned out that while the boys ate and daydreamed, the animals had overgrazed on alfalfa. The goats were in severe pain and could not be saved. None of them survived—a tremendous loss for the family. Allah Ditta, ashamed of what his son had done, punished him for his mistake by sending him to school.

In the village where my father was raised, school was for useless boys, a place for those who couldn't contribute to their family's livelihood. It was a complete disgrace for a boy my father's age. Boys were expected to have honor, a child's version of their fathers'. They were expected never to cry or show signs of hunger, to carry heavy things and fix problems around the house, to escort and safeguard their sisters (the honor of their fathers), and to help put food on the table. Being sent to school was shameful because it indicated weakness and an inability to earn income.

But my father's disgrace would one day become the reason for the education of his six daughters and the prosperity of countless women and men across Pakistan.

From the moment my father first opened a textbook to learn to read, the world suddenly expanded for him. Being the first in his family to go to school, he soon discovered what an incredible treasure they had all missed. His shame and disappointment were replaced with an urgency—an unquenchable thirst—and a lifelong determination to become a man who could help not just his family but his community, and to change some of the systems he disliked so much.

My father set goals for each year, each month, and each day to study and to read and to learn. On hot nights he often sat with a candle and a book under the enormous water pot stand, because that was the coolest place. On days he knew he would be disturbed from his studies, he would walk far from his hut and sit under the trees reading about history, geography, and other cultures and traditions, his mind and heart expanding with every word, until the sun set.

CHAPTER 5

The Child Bride

NOOR JEHAN'S NEW FRIENDS AND HER LITTLE SISTERS stood below the jujube tree in her uncle's yard as she climbed up to pick the round, ripe fruit. One of her sisters would hand her a stone, and she would throw it at the branches loaded with jujubes. The girls below would run to collect the fallen fruit in their colorful scarves and rub them on their shirts before popping them into their mouths. From the top of that tree, Noor Jehan spotted a procession of women in bright and shining clothes making their way into the *haveli*.

The women sang Sindhi and Brahui songs in high-pitched voices, holding their infants to their chests, as their uneven makeup crumbled with the humidity. Their preparations had been made in haste, running off to a wedding in chaos. Women in villages have dozens of things to do before they leave for anything: prepare lunch for the whole family, fold the beds and the clothes, bathe the kids, and so on. Only after preparing everything for their husbands and children can they get ready themselves. In that haste, all they can often manage is to pat round patches of blush onto their cheeks, smear dark red lipstick on one lip so that it would spread to the other lip over the course of the day, and smudge kohl on their eyes. Makeup is not a common thing in the villages, but if someone in that village has a TV, slowly the word will spread about how makeup is necessary for women. Soon cheap makeup stalls will spring up on the street corners that older women in long veils will walk to in herds to buy for the younger ones who are not allowed to buy for themselves.

These women in their festive clothing called Noor Jehan down from her tree and ushered her to a corner of a house. Children in my culture are taught to obey elders without question. The women decorated her like a little doll. They put her in a red dress with gold embroidery that had belonged to one of her aunts. They adorned her with jewelry lent by older relatives: big earrings that pulled on her small lobes, and a necklace that sagged to her stomach. They put fragrant oil in her hair and braided her short locks. Every time she tried to move from where she sat, women came and whispered to her in a tone that she had never heard before, a tone they used with their peers and elders, as if somehow she were now like her aunts. They told her to stay put in the corner until someone told her to move.

Sitting in the corner, Noor Jehan watched the world before her shift and change. There was so much activity.

Women were preparing food, and children her age were playing in various corners of the house. She wanted to join them, but she was stuck in the corner without knowing why. Men hurried in and out, escorting guest after guest inside until the house was full. As she sat in the corner, heat enveloped her body, the gold eye shadow dropped off of her eyelids, and her small heart beat fast. Many families came to greet her. They called her the bride. Some wept when they saw her. Some wouldn't come into the room for fear of seeing her small child's face and never forgiving themselves. (She was too young!) And some told her to be brave.

Then through the corner of the tiny window in the room, she caught a glimpse of her eldest uncle and understood that what she was experiencing was serious. Her uncle's jaw quivered, and his eyes were bloodshot with tears that he quickly rubbed off as he sensed her watching him. A few moments later, silence fell as three men escorted a bearded *mullah* (religious teacher) into the room. The women who sat next to her on the dirt floor moved to another corner. He came over and sat down facing her. The *nikah* (ceremonial signing of the wedding contract) began.

After a short prayer in Arabic, the man asked three times if she, Noor Jehan, agreed to marry a man named Sikander, son of Allah Ditta. Her heart pounding, she didn't know what to say. Then her mother whispered in her ear, "Say yes, my dear one, say yes." And so she did.

After the ceremony my mother's heart grew heavy.

Something had happened, something drastic that she did not understand and that nobody had explained to her. She would never again be a child. In that moment she didn't even feel human. She had been a bride, she realized, and now she was a wife. This had been a wedding, and she was now married. She did not want this. But she had not been given the choice.

As evening fell, the wedding procession took her to her groom's house, and the bride for whom she was being exchanged was brought into that very home. Then my mother's tears wouldn't stop. She cried and cried, begging to go back to her mother, but the women only wept as they saw her, and the men acted as if she didn't exist. Her friends were not there to tell her stories of their games or to bring their new clay toy to her. She was a wife now, to a boy whom she had not even met.

THAT NIGHT AFTER the celebrations ended, Noor Jehan was scooped up and put on a cot with a colorful *rili* and a pillow in a tiny room inside the house of a husband she still had not seen. As she sat there looking around the dark room with her teary eyes, she heard a group of girls coming to her. They were all laughing, teasing someone in their midst. It was Sikander, her new husband. Finally they sent him in and closed the door behind him, giving him the flashlight one of them was holding. There being no electricity, he took it from them. In the pale light he could see that his tiny bride was shivering. It wasn't cold. Although he was only thirteen and angry at what had just happened to him, his heart instantly filled with pity for this skinny girl with dried-up makeup streaked with tears. The silence was thick between them. They were two children in a room meant for adults. He lay down next to her, as the men had instructed him. But instead of following their other instructions, instructions for men of a certain age, he instinctively sensed her vulnerability. And he asked her a question. To this day, my mother remembers and cherishes this moment.

"Do you go to school?"

"No, I have never been," she said timidly.

Wanting to relieve their mutual anxiety, he kept talking. "What does your father do?"

"He rides a donkey cart around town and earns money by taking people from one place to another," she said in a small voice, still shaking. Neither knew what to do. They were both new at this.

Lying side by side, the newlyweds kept talking, long into the night, until they finally fell asleep. The next morning Sikander showed his new wife the drawings he'd made with the crayons his older brother had given him. She was fascinated. The difficulty and sadness of the day before had lifted some, and her curiosity awakened. She asked her new husband questions about the drawings, about the pens and colors and paint that his elder brother had given him. He brought out an old rusty metal chest and opened it to show her his storybooks. He kept them there safe, away from rain and mud.

Her eyes widened with wonder. At this moment, Sikander and Noor Jehan were not husband and wife but friends enduring a similar fate. They both had become victims to the customs of their culture, yet they were learning to find solace within each other by sharing experiences. Two children, two stories, were becoming one.

CHAPTER 6

Romance in the Village

MY PARENTS FOUND COMFORT AND FRIENDSHIP IN their shared trauma. They enjoyed each other's company even as they shared uncertainty about what would come next. They were both so young at the time of their marriage that their age was controversial even in the village where they lived. And Noor Jehan was so small and feeble. These facts brought unexpected attention to their families.

Yet the two became inseparable friends. People were gossiping about the pair in unhealthy ways, so my father's family decided to send Noor Jehan back to her family for at least a year so she could return to her husband at puberty. But by now their friendship had blossomed to the point that Sikander didn't want to be without this companion who shared his curiosity about the world. The decision to separate them angered him, even as he knew he had to abide by it as he had endured all the other decisions made for him by his elders.

Somehow the injustice of himself and his little bride being used as pawns in an ancient custom made him determined to change his lot. He saw education as his only chance at a different life. In his world of predetermined outcomes, where every aspect of his life had already been chosen for him, education was the only wild card. He began by seeking help from his best friend, Azim. They had been classmates in their small village. Azim came from a family of greater means and education than my father. He now lived in Jamshoro, Sindh, a small town famous for its educational institutions, close to the city of Hyderabad. Azim offered my father a place in his home in Jamshoro. My father took him up on the offer. He left his village and his family and went to live with his friend and pursue his dream of getting an education. For two years he slept in a barn and took his meals with Azim's family. His determination, intellect, and thirst for knowledge were so great that he worked his way through intermediate education at Sindh University, one of the acclaimed government institutions in Sindh Province.

When my mother reached the age of twelve, she was considered fully adult and went back to her husband's house—a married woman with many responsibilities. While my father was away in Jamshoro, she would rise early in the morning with her sisters-in-law, and together they would clean, cook, wash dishes, and feed the cows and the donkeys. When the sun was high in the sky, they would make cow dung patties for fuel. They gathered the warm, grassy dung, scooping it up in their right hands, rolling it between their palms before slinging it against the sun-drenched wall of the house for it to bake. It smelled like earth and made a satisfying *thwap* when it hit the wall.

Noor Jehan worked hard, but she was small, and the work was sometimes overwhelming. At times her fragile hands were unable to pick up a big stack of dishes after she washed and cleaned them, and she would fall on the wet dirt. The dishes would scatter and roll and have to be washed all over again. Once when she was trying to feed the donkey, she slipped under it. The frantic animal kicked, jumped, and brayed. Just before its powerful hooves stomped and crushed her small body, she managed to catch its gaze and stare straight up at it. By some miracle this calmed it down, and she was able to escape.

The foreign house, the new people, and the strange new responsibilities had made her afraid. She was afraid to make mistakes and afraid to disappoint anyone, especially her parents who had left her there. A daughter reflects the honor of her family, and a daughter-in-law is expected to bring a good name to her parents and her tribe. This meant showing how good she was at cooking, cleaning, embroidery, and saying yes to her mother-in-law in every instruction given to her. She was, however, the most afraid of her father-in-law. He was a strict man. He would shout at my mother for her clumsiness or slow pace and scolded her as *mai!* (woman!) when he was angry. Only then would her mother-in-law gently guide her, slowly showing her how not to stand out and how to do the work that needed to be done. Slowly my mother found her place in the family.

Meanwhile, as Sikander studied at Sindh University, he was beginning to resent his situation and became rebellious. For the first time, he encountered new ideas and ways of thinking. Being surrounded by a wider range of voices and opinions made him realize how limited his life had been in the village. He was particularly astonished to find that women pursued education alongside men, for in his youth he had never witnessed a woman holding a book, let alone debating some of the country's most crucial political issues. And he began to be inspired by, and felt drawn to, a girl from the women's dorm next to his who came from an educated, Sindhi-speaking family. In class, she asked the professor challenging questions that amazed everyone. My father wanted to marry her and make a new and better life with her.

But as soon as my father resolved to seek this woman's hand, God planted in his heart and mind the image of his child bride, that nine-year-old girl in her red bridal dress borrowed from another woman, crying at her wedding. It was not her fault that she was married to him. He realized that if an educated mind was what he loved about a woman, he could go back and educate his young wife, to help *her* read and learn about the world. Maybe they would even grow closer.

And so, with excitement and new resolve, my father returned to the village, bringing books and pens for my mother, who, at twelve, was growing up to be a beautiful young woman. As he sat among his family, who were beaming with happiness at his return, she shyly brought him water in a glass, and he couldn't help but feel the connection that they had developed that first night when they lay on their cot talking.

In a traditional Pakistani wedding, after the *nikah*, a playful ritual is performed that makes the girls giggle and even flushes the faces of the boys. This "scandalous" part of a wedding celebration is often the first time the newlyweds have any physical interaction. First the bride and groom shake hands, and then a big bowl of rice grains is placed between them. The groom scoops some rice in his hands and slowly pours it into the hands of his bride. She then pours the grains back into his, and so on. This tradition is to show that they will work together to make a home, that they will take care of each other and feed each other, hence building a promise of mutual honor for their marriage and doing nothing to betray that honor. In the end, after sharing the handful of rice back and forth, the bride lets the rice fall into the bowl. Then the groom takes out a handkerchief and wipes the hands of his bride as chants of *zal mazur* (servant of the wife) fill the air. It is a proud moment, even as the groom pretends to be ashamed, but he continues to clean the bride's hands. The bride, feeling loved and respected, glows even more radiant than before. Tragically, for some rural brides, this traditional act is the first and only time they receive such respect from their husbands.

Sikander and Noor Jehan were different. Their romantic life started not with rice sharing but at the moment when he held her hand and helped her write her first words. It began when my father taught her the English translation of a word, or gave her books to read, her face so red from shyness that she could not look him in the eye.

Their love story became a topic of discussion in the village. The gossiping women both teased my mother and envied her. Rumors of *zal mazur* started circulating among the men of the village when my parents were seen together learning. "Look at Sikander putting all his attention on his wife. He should rather put on bangles and sit with her giggling!" they would joke over chai. My father was officially a servant of his wife and proud of it. But in a society where there are accepted understandings about what is correct gender-specific behavior and what is not, gossip can be harmful. Men would say, "We too like our wives, but we don't make embroidery with them." My mother and father became aware that all eyes were on them, so they tried to keep their interactions as secret as possible.

After my mother finished her morning work in the house, and when the sun was bright in the sky, she would sit down next to my father and the lessons would begin. ABCs, *Alif, Ba, Pa,* and soon my mother was learning words! She could identify letters from the pieces of newspaper that flew in the wind and excitedly read them to my father. As soon as she learned to read, she fell in love with books. These were not big, fancy books, but early language-learning books or children's storybooks, made on thin paper, and some were secondhand books my father had found at the bazaar. She read books in Sindhi and Urdu, and she even strained to read some printed in English.

They tried hard not to make it too obvious, but their love was flourishing every day as they learned. The bond they shared was oblivious to strict traditions. My parents' love for each other would later become a big part of our own story-telling at home. When the electricity would fail, my siblings and I would sit around them as my father told stories of his childhood, with my mother snuggled up right next to him.

CHAPTER 7

A Matter of Honor

BUT THE YOUNG LOVE OF MY PARENTS WOULD SOON face a huge obstacle, something that no one could have prepared them for.

Allah Ditta was weak from illness, and his sons weren't making enough from sharecropping in the fields. The floods of 1983 had destroyed so much cropland in the area that their income opportunities decreased dramatically. His sons tried their luck at shopkeeping, herding, and paving houses or making bricks for a wage. Along with getting his education, Sikander ran a little shop in the village to earn money for his father. But nothing worked. The family suddenly became very poor and had to take loans just to feed the people in the house. So Bhalla Aba decided that his eldest son would go to Kotri, a small community outside the city of Hyderabad in Sindh, about three hundred kilometers from their hut in Larkana, where he had purchased the partially walled property that would become our *haveli*. He wanted Liaqat to build a shop on the land before anyone else could snatch it.

And so Liaqat and his wife were sent off with their few belongings in a round heap atop his wife's head.

Not until years later would I learn what exactly happened afterward. My cousins and I would sit huddled in the corner of the very *haveli* where my *kaka* (uncle) Liaqat had moved, pouring water over dried dirt to make clay as we told one another stories. With our tiny fingers, we would carefully take small chunks and shape them into faces and little bodies, while innocently telling one another the secrets we knew. Now when I look back, I realize that I made my life's biggest discoveries during those huddled playtimes. As the clay caked in our hands and we rolled it into balls in our palms, one of my cousins told me that Uncle Liaqat had beaten his wife to death.

I knew Liaqat Ali as a scary man. Silence fell whenever he entered a room. Women who had been mindlessly cleaning around the house would run for their headscarves. Children would turn mute. Men would stand up to greet him. His booming voice, his thinning hair, and his fierce big eyes, at times bloodshot from lack of sleep, could make anyone tremble. And so years later, when we children whispered about him beating his wife to death, I could imagine his big hands rising in the air and coming down with full force on my aunt's face. She would have had to stay quiet the whole time. In his loud voice, he would have shouted words of disgust, sometimes throwing in curse words in Sindhi. With his broad shoulders, tall features, and fierce eyes, Liaqat Ali didn't listen to anyone but his father.

Upon receiving word of the murder, Bhalla Aba ordered the whole family to move to Kotri. They gathered whatever they could. Liaqat was arrested, and the family scrambled to get him out of jail. Liaqat declared he had committed the murder out of sheer anger. And under the Pakistan Penal Code 300, he was set free.

When I first heard this story, it felt distant from me, almost impossible. I imagined it like something that had happened in another time, far away. Little did I know that a bigger tragedy awaited me in the years ahead.

The year before I was born, my uncle Liaqat had declared that he would marry again. He convinced Bhalla Aba to have my father agree to give *me* as an exchange bride to a tribe that lived back in the village, in order to bring him a second wife. My grandfather, who knew of his eldest son's temper and naïvely believed that a wife's care would help him, came to my young father to order him to give his first daughter (me) in *phidi,* to be betrothed before I was even born. This demand, my father realized, was one he could not honor. His duty as a son weighed heavily on him, but the tremendous injustice of such a request and its circumstances would be too much for him to bear. He had himself been victim to elders callously deciding his fate and that of his child bride. He knew the hardships. And he refused to let his daughter ever become part of this cycle of cruelty. It was the first time he raised his voice to his father, the first time he spoke up and said no, and the first time he saw his father's eyes tear up with the shame of having a disobedient son. As my father tells me today, it was the hardest thing he did in his whole life and something he would never forget.

That was when he and my mother left the *haveli* and that life to start a new one on their own, hoping to grow a family far from traditional crimes and restrictions.

To this day, I wonder what would have happened if my father had stayed, if like every son in that tribe, he had respected his father's command. That day, a year before my birth, he did the most sinful thing he could imagine: he made his father cry by raising his voice to him. But to me, standing up for a daughter he had not yet even held in his hands was the most honorable thing. He saved my life.

CHAPTER 8

A New Beginning

IN 1988, WHEN MY MOTHER WAS THIRTEEN, SHE GAVE birth to her first child in the small mud room of our *haveli* in Balochistan. According to our tradition, it was in the presence of her mother and an elderly midwife. It was a boy! My father was working as a small-time journalist at a Sindhi newspaper in Hyderabad at the time. He worked hard and he was quite good at his job, but he was still able to bring in only some six hundred PKR (Pakistani rupees, the equivalent of six dollars) to the house each month. Even with his work, there were days when he and my mother had to collect old newspapers and cardboard to sell to the recycling man in town in order to buy rice or potatoes for meals. Still, they were happy. Like any young couple, they knew they had started on a journey that the two of them would figure out together as a team. Because of their poverty, the newborn was severely malnourished and desperately needed a blood transfusion to survive. My parents could hardly afford this, and in places like Hyderabad, preferential treatment is always given to those who can afford it. In an act of desperation and ingenuity, my father tapped his small network of journalist friends and put together a radio campaign to collect blood for his son's transfusion. It worked. Soon my brother Ali was in good health.

When my mother was not busy with childcare and keeping house, she was reading every book she could. Her favorite was a story about a *sughar* woman, meaning a woman who is good at everything, from cleaning house, to keeping track of budgets, to raising children. *Sughar* women were great role models. My mother wanted to be just like them, and eventually she was. She became the woman in our neighborhood to go to for haircuts, for sewn dresses, and for traditional ear and nose piercings. She was even consulted for advice on putting together a savings club for the local women.

Only a year later, at the age of fourteen, my mother had me. Being a small girl still herself, she was weak when I was born. I was tiny, like a little chick with pale skin and bones that could be broken if someone held me too tight. Just like my brother, I was severely malnourished, but my condition was more severe because of the diarrhea that I had from birth. I quickly became extremely dehydrated.

Within two weeks I became so frail and blue in the body that no one had any hope for my survival. They took me to many doctors, but none of them knew what to do with me. One day my aunts came to visit, to see my young mother and her ailing infant. They held me in their arms and cried. Together they mourned me.

That was when—out of core indigenous belief—they

decided to change my name. It is said that names can sometimes impact us negatively when they run against our character. My tribe believes that a name that matches our personality helps us feel lighter and stronger. Conversely, a wrong name can weigh us down and make us weak. My original name had been Zubaida. Now, together with my aunts, my mother decided to name me Khalida.

The indigenous wisdom of my aunts worked where conventional medical knowledge failed. I not only survived but was soon on the road to recovery. Somehow the combination of those women's faith in God, trust in intuition, and tribal wisdom cured me. My name is a reflection of that faith, and I honor it everywhere I go. We would later come to learn that Khalida means "immortal."

I GREW UP TO be Aba's little girl with two ponytails. When I was small, my father loved putting me on his shoulders and taking me outside. This was very unusual, as in my culture fathers do this only with their sons. I would hold tight to his hair as he walked. I loved the way the world looked from up high, the way my mother must have viewed it from the branches of her pomegranate tree back home. As Aba walked past, people stared at us, witnessing this strange bond of father and daughter. We passed shops, donkey carts, and cars. Some people would wave at me, and I would grin with pride, my tiny feet kicking my father's shoulders. Later I would come to believe that Aba carried me on his shoulders to show everyone how special I was to him, and for me to see that my place was up above cultural restrictions. Rules couldn't pull me down from my place in the world.

To give my brother and me a good life, Aba sometimes worked three different jobs in a single day, while Ammi (Mommy) sewed dresses and pierced ears from home. They never let us feel what poverty meant. Aba would take Ali and me for outings on his motorcycle after he returned from work at night. We would sing songs while holding each other on the back of his bike as he drove fast in the streets of Hyderabad.

When my sister Fatima arrived, we children began to overwhelm our seventeen-year-old mother while Aba was at the office. So Aba had a great idea: he would drop us off at the local library before he went to work. Although we couldn't actually read yet, we loved it—the smell of books, row after row of information, stories, magic, and wonder. I would fly from shelf to shelf, hunting for the books with the pop-ups, while Fatima would play with an abacus, content-edly adding and subtracting beads from each wire. (Years later she would pursue a degree in business administration.) And Ali would concentrate on one book at a time, diligently looking at it, enraptured.

Books were a big part of our lives. Some of my favorite memories are of my father taking us to get used books from a small roadside shack close to the city center in Hyder-abad. He valued books so much that when friends and family came to visit us in our empty apartment, they would joke that we should make furniture from all the books.

We moved many times while in Hyderabad, mostly when my father could no longer afford the rent. I had fun lugging our small load of possessions (mostly books) to a new house in rice sacks and bundled in scarves, blissfully unaware of the stress my parents must have been feeling. One of my favorite houses was in Bhitai Town, a small, well-built area on the outskirts of Hyderabad. It had a big jujube tree in the courtyard that was so tall, we could reach the berries only from the roof. Bhitai Town was where my father first made known his desire that I become a doctor. One of our neighbors was a rich Sindhi woman. My mother and aunts called her Appa ("Elder Sister" in Urdu). When she discovered my mother's talents in embroidery, Appa paid her to make blankets and quilts. Appa often invited us to her house, where we sat on plush sofas while a decorated fan spun above our heads. This was a novelty to us, as we sat on woven straw mats at home. Appa bragged about her daughter, who served us chai and biscuits and sweets like *gulab jamun* (balls of fried chickpea dough soaked in sugar water). She sat next to us on the sofa in this tidy room, our slippers sprawled just outside the door.

My father came with us sometimes, and it was there he saw how proud Appa was of her daughter who was studying to be a doctor. He started thinking he would be proud if *I* grew up to be a doctor too. I would be able to help all my relatives who suffered from illnesses, none of whom could afford treatment in Western-style hospitals. So long before I started school, my father had decided what he wanted me to be when I grew up. And even though it wasn't what I would've chosen for myself, I took pride in it because it made my father proud.

We moved once again, and one day in our new house,

Aba and Ammi had no money to cook a meal. So we just sipped *sulaimani chai* (tea without milk) for breakfast. But that afternoon when Aba was at work, Ammi handed Ali and me some broken wooden crates to try to sell in the market outside our street. We felt very grown up and responsible. Ali and I happily made the ten-minute walk dragging the crates behind us. When we reached the place where the market connected with the road, there were so many people—men selling fruit and vegetables, some making *pakoras* (fried snacks), some waiting for a bus—that it was confusing and overwhelming. Buses were loading and unloading people, and there was trash everywhere.

We meekly went up to one of the fruit *walas,* who had many people standing nearby. Before we could ask him to buy the wood crates from us, he shouted at Ali for getting in the way. Ali was shocked and became ashamed. We quickly sold our crates for very little, bought some potatoes, and hurried home with our little hearts thumping in our chests. I will never forget the look on Ali's face: it burned with resolve never to be poor again. He would later become a successful filmmaker.

CHAPTER 9

Mornings in Kotri

My FATHER COULD NO LONGER AFFORD TO KEEP US in the city, and we had to move back to Kotri, back to the brick *haveli* that my parents had left five years earlier, near the train tracks. Most of the houses were illegally occupied, and many had no doors, only a quilt nailed over the entrance to create the illusion of privacy. Gutters of wastewater passed by each door, and dirty children played outside.

We lived with our three uncles and a dozen cousins. My cousins were some of my best friends: Kalsoom, Jameela, and Sajda. We also played with a neighbor girl named Sima and of course my sister Fatima. Over the years we did many things together, from storytelling in bed, to giggling about puberty, to taking fresh dough to a local *hotel* (restaurant) to bake our *rotis* in their *tandoor* (in-ground oven). Our mothers would sometimes send us to get milk from a nearby *waro*, a dairy farm. Kalsoom and I would walk fifteen minutes to get there, hand them our buckets made of old vegetable oil cans, and wait until they milked the cows for us. When they handed our heavy tins back, the sweet scent of fresh milk would make us hungry. The foam topped to the brim looked delicious! So she and I decided that since our moms needed only the milk, we'd better eat the froth. The whole walk back to the *haveli*, we scooped it all up with our dirty index fingers.

One of our favorite activities was to stand at the train tracks and wave at the trains as they passed, imagining where the passengers were headed. I loved seeing all the people sitting inside and peeking out through the windows. I would imagine stories for them. We would run to the tracks and stand just a few inches from the steel behemoth grumbling past, blowing hot wind, fumes, and dust into our faces as we frantically waved.

Every afternoon my friends and I would play together in the dirt. We would put rocks in old plastic bags, swing the bags in the air, and let the rocks fly free, imagining they were headed to a different world that we couldn't even visualize. Gutters connected the illegal homes of the poor community, including some immigrants from Afghanistan, and sewage from the industrial plants on the other side of the tracks made the dirt moist. Sima and I dug up the warm, wet clay and shaped it into dolls, because neither of us had real dolls. We made clay beds and sofas for them, like we had seen on TV at Appa's house. As we played, the boys played with sticks and tires nearby, laughing. Men sat outside shops, talking about a cricket match or someone's financial troubles. Women in long colorful scarves hurried past. We made fake henna tattoos out of mud and pretended to be brides.

Mornings in Kotri were delicious. We woke up early to the scent of *paratha* (fried flatbread), chai, and *khara* (flaky biscuits), with the birds chirping and a rooster calling. We would run after trucks loaded with sugarcanes and grab some to peel and suck the delicious sweet juice. In the late afternoon, we were called inside the house to have chai with everyone. The smell of milk, water, sugar, and tea, mingling with the scent of wood burning as my mother or my aunt cooked in the *haveli*'s small kitchen; these are the aromas I associate with childhood.

As I got older, I realized that some girls, like my friends Najma and Rubi, weren't allowed to play outside. Like me, they were six or seven years old, but they wore long scarves even in the house. We would sit on the floor of their modest rooms, making dolls out of cloth or playing *cham cham* (pattycake).

One of my favorite things about growing up in Kotri was the immense kindness people had for one another. Everyone was struggling, and families would help one another out whenever they could. I took pride in helping my mother cook for neighbors who had just moved in and perhaps didn't have a fire to prepare their lunch. Or we collected children from the neighborhood to give them food. And sometimes we took food next door because we knew they might not be able to afford that day's meal.

Just like that, one day in the heat of the afternoon sun, my mother gave me a cup of gravy and *roti* and asked me to take it to my friend Sima's house across the train tracks. I happily crossed the tracks and walked to the house, pushing my feet in the dirt the way I liked. I entered the house without knocking, as was my custom. I heard Sima crying, and then I saw her hugging her mother, who was also weeping. I froze, the *roti* and gravy still in my hands.

Sima's mother was being kicked out of her house. Her husband was divorcing her because she had "dishonored" him by visiting a female friend in the neighborhood without asking his permission. My mother was allowed to go out on her own; she did not have to report to my father, and he never became suspicious of what she was doing or whom she was seeing. With tears running down my eyes and nose, I ran home. I never saw Sima again.

After witnessing Sima and her mother's helplessness, I felt it important to have an education, in case my future husband did the same thing to me. I wanted to go to school as an act of rebellion more than anything else, to make myself stronger. I looked up to one person for a model of female strength—my cousin Khadija, the elder sister of Kalsoom. She was a beautiful girl several years older than me. Every morning she put on a crisp white uniform that she had washed the night before, and a long white shawl, and she carried her books in the crook of her arm. Khadija was the eldest daughter of my *kaka* Ali, my uncle on my father's side. Perhaps because she was the eldest daughter, or perhaps because her fair skin and big eyes made her the center of everyone's attention, she grew up to be self-confident, carrying herself with a great sense of pride. In cloistered, traditional village life, many interpret these features as signs of arrogance, but I looked up to Khadija with admiration and affection. I thought of her as an elder sister. I was captivated by the way she could be so silent and serious; she could gaze at you with a look that was so piercing, it seemed to be searching your very soul.

People wagged their tongues when Khadija showed her love for education and fought to go to school. She was often seen reading a magazine or writing: people gossiped that now that she was educated, she wrote love poems. As the eldest of five sisters, she had started the revolution of education but was opposed not only by her community but by her own family.

One day her mother (my aunt) put on Khadija's school scarf while she washed dishes. Khadija asked her to take it off. It was her only scarf for school, and she took pride in wearing clean, crisp clothes. Her mother didn't respond, intending to embarrass her. Khadija pleaded with her mother, who picked up the end of her scarf and cleaned her dirty teeth with it, yellowing it, proving her dislike for Khadija's schooling. Khadija's eyes filled with tears. Her mother felt immense peer pressure from her neighbors and her family to put her daughter in her place, but Khadija was resolved to rise above it.

CHAPTER 10

A Street Kid

THE NEXT YEAR ABA HAD FINALLY SAVED ENOUGH money to move us back to Hyderabad and educate us. He invited one male family member each from his and Ammi's families to live with us and go to school with us.

My first school was a government school where the boys wore dark yellow uniforms and the girls wore sky-blue-and-white dresses. But because I was the only girl in my class, I was allowed to wear whatever I wanted. Throughout my childhood I enjoyed wearing my traditional Brahui dress with the pocket in the front (which I always believed was there so you could keep your favorite things close to you). I wear these traditional dresses to this day.

My favorite part of going to school was the long walk to get there. My cousins and I would climb over small sand dunes, pass through markets, even through the main hall of a local hospital, and finally make our way through a fancy mall. I liked to look through the glass windows of the closed shops, especially a fancy toy shop that had dolls lined up on the shelves. I had only ever had my own handmade clay dolls, so when I saw a doll with two hearts on her cheeks, my heart exploded. She was plump and white-skinned, with big eyes. I wanted that doll so badly; I wanted to hold her and cradle her like a baby.

I was a good student, and the teachers liked me. The boys were naughty, always pulling pranks on one another, but they didn't dare say anything to me because I came to school with two boy cousins and a brother. At home, Ammi and Aba both took an interest in our schoolwork, asking questions and helping out. Aba used to give us homework himself. We had to write paragraphs from a chapter of our book on our black slates. We did it dozens of times to perfect our handwriting.

Ammi and Aba always made sure we had time to do our homework, but because I was the elder daughter, I had the most responsibilities around the house. Fatima was still too little to help, and Ali was a boy. I did not like this. *"Shonki!"* my mother would call (meaning someone who wants too many things), asking me to wash the dishes or the clothes or clean the floors. I often cut the vegetables for Ammi to cook, cleaned the rice of small stones, wiped down the stairs, bathed the children, and scrubbed the dirty diapers. Sometimes I quarreled with my mother, refused to work, and hid in a corner to sulk.

Then my father would come home and ask, "Where is my Khali?" My mother would angrily point to the corner where I was hiding. He'd bring me out on his shoulders.

"She does not like doing house chores. What will happen to her when she grows up?" Ammi would ask.

"What will happen? Nothing at all," Aba said. "My daughter won't have to do any of these chores. When she is older, she will be a leader, and others will do her chores." This would instantly make me smile.

Ammi enrolled me in a mosque on our street that was for female students only and run by women. I proudly called myself a *talib* (student), part of a *taliban* (group of students). Back at the *haveli*, some cute boys would come at noon every day to ask for food. They would knock on the door, and you would ask who was there, and a small, cute voice would say, *"Talib!"* It was more like they sang it to you, and everyone would *aww* over them. My aunts would pour a ladleful of that day's meal onto their plate, which already had food from the other neighbors. Always modest, some would make potatoes, some lentils, some would just boil a few vegetables. We often made the same, except for Thursdays, when Bhalla Aba would bring meat.

This woman-led mosque in Hyderabad was where I learned about the many beauties of Islam: the four most important prophets (Muhammad P.B.U.H. [peace be upon him], Moses, Jesus, and David, peace be upon them all), the angels, the presence of God, and the freedom that religion provides. Beginning with the first grades at school, we learned how to be Muslims and live a virtuous life. We learned that Islam says no one should hold anger, greed, or dishonesty and distrust in the heart, because the heart is the house of God and should not be polluted by such thoughts. Whenever we feel such emotions, it means Satan has taken over us and is impairing our judgment, and we must recite this special verse, *La hawla wala quwwata illa bil-*

lah, "There is no power, no strength, greater than Allah," to rid ourselves of this unholy influence.

I was fascinated! I shared everything I learned with everyone: my cousins, who were never able to attend school; my friends, some of whom were given off into marriage at young ages; and my aunts, who behind closed doors read the Holy Quran in Arabic by sounding the letters aloud, having no idea what the words meant. When I repeated what I had learned about Satan grasping our hearts, the women told me that the most obvious times Satan grasps our hearts is when we have feelings of romance or love for a boy. If I ever felt like a certain boy looked nice or if I wanted to talk to him, I should quickly recite the verse I had learned in order to eradicate Satan. It could be dangerous to fall in love.

The next year, when we were in Kotri for the Eid celebration, I was playing with Kalsoom in the unfinished room at the end of the *haveli.* I had just made a clay doll that was drying in the sun. Kalsoom went out for something, and her sister Khadija came into the room. We were alone. "Khalida," she whispered, "what is it you were saying that people recite when Satan takes you over?" In my childish innocence, I mindlessly repeated the verse I had been taught: "There is no power, no strength, greater than Allah." I was too naïve to think about why she was asking me, and I went on cheerfully playing with my doll. I later saw this innocent moment as a turning point for me and my family, and knowing that it could have unfolded differently, I would regret it for the rest of my life.

CHAPTER 11

My Heart Belongs
to the Mountains

Balochistan was where my spirit belonged. Whenever I knew we were going back to our *haveli* there, for summer or winter breaks, I couldn't sleep out of anticipation and happiness. It took us many days to prepare for this trip, which would take about twelve hours. We put old clothes and shoes in a gunny sack to take to the poor. We washed and laid out our own clothes and wrapped them in a *dupatta* (headscarf) or a plastic bag. I put on my favorite dress, even though it would be filthy by the time we arrived.

First we took a bus from Hyderabad to Karachi, where we would transfer to another for the journey to Khuzdar in Balochistan. The first ride lasted about three hours, and it was dark by the time we reached Karachi. My sister Fatima and I were groggy, our hair frizzy, but our chests throbbed with excitement, knowing that we would soon see our beautiful mountains. In Karachi we bought chips, juice, and *chole chaat* (spicy chickpeas with onions and spices in a small plastic bag), for the long trip ahead.

I loved the hustle and clamor of the bus. The luggage was tied up top, and when there was no more room on the roof, things would come inside: sacks of rice and lentils, or a basket with five chickens in it. Sometimes a goat was allowed to walk to and fro in the aisle. Men smoked cigarettes and women fussed over children. Eighties Bollywood music blared at top volume. When the bus started moving, my mother would say a prayer loudly, *Bismillah* (Begin in the name of Allah), and hold her veil up to her face. We were off to the part of the world I loved most.

When we arrived in Khuzdar, we took a donkey cart from the station to the *haveli* of my mother's family. The tall mountains, the dry land, the multicolored rocks and boulders of this province made my heart sing. The family *haveli* was a single-story compound made of hand-caked mud and cow dung that often dissolved in heavy rains. Many times I watched my uncles working on a new room. They would make big, perfectly round bricks of wet clay and arrange them in a straight line on top of one another to make walls.

During the summers in Balochistan, Fatima and I would hear the bell of the *chole* cart, and our ears would perk up. The man tinkling the bell was walking slowly down the street, pushing his wooden cart with a big steaming pot of *chole*, calling, *"Chole wala! Chole wala!"* For a rupee, he would give *chole* in a small clear plastic bag, tied with a thread. You had to make a hole in the corner to eat it from the side. The warm spicy *chole* had rich flavors that you wanted to savor. We would take about an hour to finish one plastic bag full of *chole*.

Throughout my joyous childhood, I was deeply conscious of the fact that I was privileged. I went to school, held books, and was able to read. The contrast between my urban world and this world of the mountain village sometimes bothered me, as my little cousins went about the house washing dishes and doing laundry. The distinction between childhood and adulthood was all but nonexistent for these families, and there was certainly no such thing as adolescence. My siblings and I were lucky enough to have parents who saw us as more than just another pair of hands. They made us work in the house but never expected us to earn money for the family.

Almost out of guilt, I would try to make it up to my cousins by gathering them together and reading aloud from my big book of Grimm's fairy tales. I read the stories of Hansel and Gretel, of Tom Thumb and Rapunzel. In my child's voice, I translated every sentence from English to Brahui, our indigenous language. It was uncommon for a girl like me to be able to read English, and I felt powerful and knowledgeable, grateful for the freedoms I enjoyed.

Playing with clay dolls was my favorite thing to do in Balochistan. A group of eight of us (including boy cousins) would imagine and enact wedding celebrations with them. But each year when I returned, I would find that one or more of the girls had been married at age ten or eleven. I didn't understand most of it, but I could see they were not happy. They had to leave their mothers' homes to go live in the mountains with their new husbands. In the summers their husbands would bring them to see their mothers, and I would visit with these girls. I saw their new grown-up attitudes, their sad faces, and their inability to play. They were now considered women, no longer just enjoying being children.

In the distant mountains of Kharzan, where some of my great-uncles lived, I had a best friend named Gudi. Each time we visited, she and I would go to our favorite place in the mountains—a small hill with a beautiful little pond, the remnant of flash floods, when the river receded and left water stranded in the rocks. We would jump into it. One summer Gudi tried to show me how to swim. I never fully learned (until my husband taught me years later) because I was afraid of the deep water and the slimy rocks beneath my feet. Gudi, however, would dunk herself in the water, telling me it was fine. While I lingered on the rocks, scared of even putting my feet in the water, she would laugh, and her laughter would echo through the canyon.

The next year when I returned, Gudi was married off. She had been sent away to the mountains without any trace. I cried for days. People told me that she had respected her family's decision by getting married at a young age, and hence she had raised the honor of the family and her father. It broke my heart and ate at my soul. When I returned to city life, my sadness still had not left me.

CHAPTER 12

The Overnight Adult

WHEN I WAS TEN, WE MOVED TO KARACHI, WHERE my father had taken a job as a university researcher. It was a sprawling city, thronged with tens of millions of people. Cars, buses, motorcycles, and donkey carts all cramped together on the small roads, while vendors sold coloring books, pens, street food, and live goats. Women in burqas, in *shalwar qameez* (long shirts over loose pants, the traditional outfit for both women and men), or even in jeans strolled past beggars who stopped everyone for money in the name of God. Smoke came from the cars, from the barbecued chicken tikka on the carts, and from the waste burning on the roadsides.

The neighborhood of Gizri was much more congested than any place we'd ever lived, but somehow it felt like home. Kids played outside all day long. People spoke Brahui. Men sat on the street corners talking with laughter and warmth. Women walked to the markets. There was a sense of community and pride.

But one thing I soon discovered about Karachi was its modern conservatives. In the villages women went to fetch water and worked in the fields with men, but in the city, women and girls who lived in the lower middle class had much more restricted lives. Brothers and fathers took note of everywhere they went and what they did. They had to ask permission for everything—to visit a friend or even to walk across the street—and many times they were denied. Everything was about what other men would say if they saw this or heard that.

One afternoon my sister Fatima, my younger brother Sajjad, and I were outside throwing a ball around, shouting and happy. At one point Sajjad threw the ball toward me, and I ran for it, but it fell near three men who were talking at the end of the street. The men looked absorbed in their conversation. I picked up the ball.

But soon Ammi called me inside the house.

A neighbor woman had seen me pick up the ball near the men and had come over to our little house, draped in a long shawl. She introduced herself and said she had seen me "near the men." Her tone made it seem ugly and criminal. A cloud of worry came over Ammi's young face. She sat the woman down and made chai for her and told me to wash the dishes that were piled up in the corner. I frowned but picked up the water hose to fill a bucket. (Water was scarcer here than it had been in Hyderabad, and we had to use it sparingly.) Later that evening I saw Ammi talking to Aba.

I was confused. *Why did my mother call me in from our game? Why is today different from any other day?* It turned out, the woman had come to tell my mother that I was too old to play in the streets. At thirteen, I was almost a woman, and the men had been watching me. Suddenly my parents were worried. In struggling to educate their children and meet their basic needs, they had not thought about what young adulthood would mean, especially for their daughters. Suddenly they saw differences in me that they hadn't seemed to notice before. The little rise on my chest, the flush on my cheeks. My few inches of greater height were suddenly disconcerting.

Soon after that Aba told me I had to sit differently on the motorcycle when I rode with him. I had to ride like a woman, dangling both legs on one side, instead of straddling the seat comfortably, as he did and as I had always done behind him, wrapping my arms around his waist. It was painful to watch him try to explain why I had to sit this new way. He was awkward in a way I'd never seen before, searching for the words.

He finally called to my mother, who came to the door. "Bibi," he said, "don't you think now our daughter should start sitting like this?" My mother immediately understood. It was inappropriate for girls to sit with their legs open on a bike, and it occurred to me that this was why no girls had bicycles or motorcycles. I did what was asked of me and started sitting like a woman, with only one hand on Aba's shoulder. When the wind touched my face and hair, it no longer brought me the happy feeling of freedom that it once had.

That August, on Pakistan's Independence Day, Fatima and I were about to leave for our school party. We were dressed up in the matching new light green *lehengas* (long skirts) that Ammi had sewn for us. I was standing outside combing my hair when I felt Aba nudge me. Frowning, he told me to go inside because the men working on the electricity tower could see me and my hair. I was shocked! I looked up toward the workers, who were staring at me with expressions that made me feel nauseous.

Another time one of my aunts came to visit and said to my mother, "Bibi! You must teach your daughter many things now. Look at her, she is almost a woman!" My aunt stared right at my chest. From that day forward, Ammi made me wear my scarf so that it covered my chest at all times, down to my elbows.

The year I was thirteen, I got my period. When I first saw the blood, I was terrified. As a child, I had seen an aunt give birth, and at this time I thought just being in the same room as a boy could get you pregnant, so I believed I was giving birth. Living as we did far from our tribe, nobody had explained things to me. I was an experiment, a source of weird wisdom for my parents that sometimes made them second-guess things. Looking back, I think they were so afraid of making a mistake, so afraid I might act in a way that would cause the tribe to question the freedom they had given to me and my sisters that they kept me in the dark about many things.

I panicked. How challenging it was to be a woman! How difficult life was when you were unable to speak openly! So I kept quiet, convinced I had brought shame upon my family. I went to the bathroom several times a day to clean up, but one day a silk shirt I loved was stained red.

Ammi came running from the kitchen and took me into a room. I assumed she was angry and that I was facing punishment. I thought I could be killed for the serious dishonor of having a baby without a husband. But as she explained, "It happens to all the women, it's natural," relief washed over me.

As I recovered my senses, my mother tried to look into my eyes. Her crooked smile couldn't hide the fear that filled them. In her experience, when a mother finds out that her daughter is menstruating, the next day the family is supposed to look for a husband for her if she is not already betrothed. If my parents had honored the stipulations of the *wata sata* exchange, and if my father had not moved out of the village when he did, I would soon be married to another man to bring my uncle Liaqat a wife.

In my tribe's world, when Muhammad P.B.U.H. said, "Fulfill your duties to your children when they are *baligh* [mature]," it meant marrying the daughters off the moment they bled. But by *baligh*, Muhammad P.B.U.H. really meant the age when children are capable of fulfilling their duties and responsibilities as grown adults.

In that instant, my heart went out to my mother. I could not blame her for her fears. I understood the difficulties we had yet to face. Daughters are a blessing from God, but they are a tough gift to cherish. Everyone wants a piece of them. Always.

CHAPTER 13

A Question of Honor

AROUND THE TIME THAT I SHOWED PHYSICAL SIGNS of crossing the threshold from girlhood into womanhood, something happened to the cousin I loved dearly, something that turned my world upside down and set me on my path to effect change in my culture.

On one of our trips to Kotri, I noticed that Khadija was nowhere to be found. The house was as dark as night inside, the air thick and musty. We sat out in the courtyard under flickering stars; the dim light of the yellow bulb hanging from a ragged cord glowed against the brick wall. Women spoke in whispers. Some men were sleeping on cots, while others just stared straight ahead. Then two of my childhood friends and the daughters of my second uncle snuggled up with me on one *khat* (wooden jute bed) with blankets. To our right was the children's *khat* with the younger kids under the *rilis*. They poked their heads out from beneath the colorful patterns and whispered to one another, giggling sometimes.

I worked up the nerve to ask what had happened, what was eating everyone alive. My friends on the *khat* would tell me nothing. When I asked, they looked at each other, perhaps thinking I was a fragile city girl who couldn't handle the hard truths of rural, tribal life. I wondered: *Had Khadija been married off? But then why the silence? Perhaps she had fallen ill, and they had hidden her away for the traditional forty days. Or had she died of some extreme illness?*

Two kids on the *khat* next to ours heard my questions. The younger one, who had night blindness, came toward me, her arms stretched out in front of her into the darkness.

"They have killed her," she said, in a voice that was hoarse and adult-like. "Because she did something bad, they killed her."

My world stood still in that moment. The soft sounds, shadows, and lights disappeared, making way for a thick darkness as I tried to grasp what I had just heard. I don't remember falling asleep that night, but I do remember the feeling that everything was happening very quickly. It was as if ghosts descended upon me in my safe and known world. Although I had known of honor killings before, they had always been at a remove, never touching me directly. This moment of registering Khadija's death marked the end of my innocence, and it raised questions I would struggle with for the rest of my life.

IN THE DAYS THAT FOLLOWED, I began to piece together Khadija's story, but it would take many years to learn the full truth. One insidious thing about honor killings is that their purpose is to destroy not just the body but also the soul, so that by forgetting her, the family can hope to restore the dignity they have lost because of her. Often after a girl is murdered, her belongings are buried or burned; friends and family are not to speak of her ever again; her name is never mentioned aloud. It is supposed to be as if she never lived.

In the years before Khadija was murdered, she and her family had moved to a village in upper Sindh that was extremely poor, but more affordable than life in Kotri. Everyone worked in the fields to receive a daily wage. There were no schools, hospitals, or even electricity. Kalsoom, her sisters, and her mother worked in the fields all day.

Khadija hated this new life and kept herself removed. She stayed home and tried to educate her sisters, and when she wasn't doing that, she would sit in the corner and compose poetry in Urdu, Pakistan's national language.

Around this time Khadija fell in love with a Sindhi boy from the neighborhood. He made her feel that she had value, that her thoughts and her beliefs mattered. He made her feel like a queen, that she could be loved and cared for. I don't know how or where they would meet. But one dark night, filled with romantic thoughts of a good life with her beloved, she put on her best dress and shoes and left home with the boy to get married. She thought they would live a happy life somewhere far away. Like many of my cousins, Khadija had been promised to a man when she was a young girl—in her case, to one of my cousins.

Quick as the blink of an eye, yet long enough to feel like decades, a roar of anger went up from the hundreds of relatives in our tribe. The gossip was so thick in the village that the family moved back to Kaka Liaqat's *haveli* in Kotri. Liaqat, who had become the head of the family after my paternal grandfather's death, immediately gathered a group of men who searched every road, every bus station, and every other place they could think of to find the couple.

It took less than a week to hunt them down.

Nobody talks about how and where they were found, so this part of the story I do not know. But the boy's family arrived immediately, to make sure no harm came to him. And my cousin was brought back to Kotri.

Kalsoom created such chaos about the cruel way her sister was being treated like a criminal that the family decided to send her to stay at her grandmother's house until a decision was made about Khadija. But Kalsoom demanded to see her sister once before she was taken there. The house where Khadija was being held was made of red brick with a dirt courtyard. In the room closest to the gate, where jute *khats* lined the wall, Khadija lay on a ragged rug. She was wrapped in blankets, staring silently at the wall. Among her five sisters, Khadija was closest to Kalsoom. Even with their three-year age difference, Khadija used to share her thoughts and worries with Kalsoom, and Kalsoom was always inspired by Khadija's continuous struggle for education.

When Kalsoom arrived at the house, the aunts greeted

her nervously and led her to Khadija. As Kalsoom held to the edge of the door, a figure came into her vision. Someone extremely thin was staring back at her from the corner of the room. There she was! Her sister, whom everyone in the world was calling a sinner, a bad woman, a *kari* (dishonored woman), the sister she loved with all her heart. "Khajo!" she called her by her nickname. Amid tears and unanswerable questions, Kalsoom and Khadija hugged and sobbed. Meanwhile in the kitchen the women in the house sat close to each other, silently holding their scarves up to their mouths as their eyes bled with sadness.

Finally Khadija, in the middle of her tears, asked, "What punishment has father decided for me?"

The answer—and the punishment—came soon. In a couple of days, three men—my uncle Liaqat and two others—arrived at the house. They took Khadija by the arm and asked her to walk beside them.

She knew immediately that she was going to be killed, as it was the only way for the family to restore their lost honor. The women in the *haveli* cried and begged the men to let her be, to forgive her sins. But Khadija stood with confidence. Wearing her chador, she walked out with them.

It was a long walk. On that day the earth, the trees, and the wind witnessed a young skinny girl walking beside three big men who knew only that they must kill. They walked for five hours, until the graveyard came into sight. There among lines of graves raised with dirt and stone, Khadija saw an empty grave dug into the earth. She knew it was hers.

And so in the year 2002, at the age of fourteen, my cousin Khadija was murdered in the name of honor. Her photos were burned. Her clothes were thrown away. Her identity was removed.

Khadija's mother would die of grief. Her father, unable to bear the burden of what he had allowed, died of a heart attack soon after. Khadija's second sister was disgraced and married off as a second wife. One of her younger sisters was taken out of school and married off. Sajda, a thirteen-year-old, disappeared from the family to avoid being married off to an older man. Kalsoom, only twelve at the time, was left to practice nursing at a local clinic and take care of the uncle who murdered Khadija, along with her two youngest siblings. The murder on that sad day in 2002 led to the death and devastation of an entire family. It left no room for honor.

I imagine that in her last moments Khadija looked around at the men and saw no gun, no sticks, no knives. Maybe she looked straight into the eyes of her uncle and asked how he planned to kill her. Her daring gaze, her confident tone, and her erect posture might have made the three men uncomfortable. But they had a job to do, and they did it.

They strangled her. And then they buried her. All because she had fallen in love.

Before all the photos of Khadija were taken away and buried or burned, I remember seeing one of them. She is with her family. Her older sisters have grim, set faces and look unprepared to be photographed, as though they've

quickly placed their scarves on their heads at the last minute, perhaps preoccupied with thoughts of food or chores.
The younger ones have dirt all over themselves.

Khadija stands in the center, her arms crossed, looking
defiantly at the camera.

Part Two

CHAPTER 14

Life After the Murder

PEOPLE OFTEN BECOME POETS WHEN THEY FALL IN LOVE, but I became a poet when hate entered my heart. My cousin had just been murdered. She was killed for something that was considered a sin: love. Murdered unjustly by my own uncle. Her father had let it happen. Her mother had had no power. The society watched as she was dragged from her home. Memories of her were erased. And we were instructed never to say her name again. *Khadija*.

That was the hardest part; the inability to speak about it. My cousin had shown me that education is power. Her confidence had inspired me. Her powerful gaze lingered in my thoughts, but now she had never existed. The pain shoved me into a new reality. For years, I had nightmares about Khadija: sudden flashes of her face staring straight at me, her eyes wide and bold. This vision also appeared to me at random times during the day. Whether I was in school or at home washing dishes, I felt that Khadija was living with me, haunting me with thoughts of what I might

have done to save her. I thought of that day two years before her murder, when my clay doll, rather than she, had
had all my attention. She had hinted at what might become of her, when she could be saved. And so when the
pain became a silent throbbing in my chest, I sat in dark
corners of rooms composing her existence into a poem. I
tried to imagine what it felt like to be a *kari*. I closed my eyes
and tried to imagine how she had felt when she realized
that her punishment was death and no one could save her.
They took her life to save honor? What kind of honor allows that?

The questions that came out of my heart became
poems, with hurt sown into each word. I wrote many in
Urdu, the language taught to us at school, trying to make
Khadija the voice of every woman and girl murdered in
the name of honor. I read my poems to Aba, who tried to
hide the cloud of concern that hovered over his face, as he
said I had grown older than my actual age. In my desperation, I asked him about honor killings. I already knew what
Islam says about such heinous acts. I had studied in the
Holy Quran that Allah forbade hurting any soul. Killing
one person is like killing the whole of mankind, God says.
There were instructions after instructions on the rights of
women in Islam and the freedoms that both men and
women share. Then what was it that led men to kill in the
name of honor? To understand that, I had to understand
the concept of dishonor and what it actually meant for
men: a state of ridicule in the society; an inability to show
face in the community; a position reinforced by a community that refuses to interact with the man who does not act

in harsh ways to preserve his honor. Some of the common explanations for honor murders are that the men weren't thinking, that they were so angry, they weren't in their right minds. But how could this be true when the murders were often planned? They were both senseless and premeditated.

I slowly learned that "honor" killings—a custom not ordered by religion, caste, or tradition but done solely to restore men's egos—weren't just my tribe's issue but took place all across Pakistan and all over the world. The shock was enough to transform my agony into action. Khadija's murder shook me to the core. It made me question my very identity, my role in my family, tribe, and society.

I always thank God that I had a father who heard me. Aba listened to my anger and understood my rage. He saw my despair. And I believe he was secretly grateful.

Aba was running a nonprofit nongovernmental organization called Participatory Development Initiatives (PDI). When big institutions like the Asian Development Bank, the IMF, and the World Bank invested in projects in Pakistan, the projects often didn't include the local communities in the planning and implementation processes. By not being sensitive to the cultural issues surrounding major infrastructure changes, these projects ended up harming the local and indigenous communities as much as helping them. Aba organized conferences and workshops on the big issues that affected local populations—water, disaster management, environmental policies, and gender rights—in order to raise awareness in those communities and engage them in the planning process, and he also organized an event at an international gathering called the World Social Forum in Karachi, where we were living at the time.

I enjoyed helping Aba with his conferences, learning what he did and how. The sight of hundreds of people convening in one place to discuss issues that were impacting communities around the world made me feel connected for the first time to something larger than myself, and I saw how this kind of work could become my path. Aba often asked me to be the announcer during these events. I began to read my poems to conference attendees so they could know the truth about honor killings. I didn't think about taking on an issue so brutal and big—I just wanted others to hear my pain in my words.

At a conference on water rights, my father made me the master of ceremonies, and I surprised the audience by pausing in my commentary and asking them to listen to a poem. It was one I'd written about Khadija. It was incredibly awkward and the audience was stunned, but they listened. In the audience were men from all kinds of tribes, traditions, and social classes. As I finished reading, I looked up and saw Aba beaming with pride.

One day in April 2006, a year after I began reading my poems to activists and civil society members, I was reading a poem in front of an audience of about eighty people. Among them were organizers for a global campaign called WE CAN End Violence Against Women. In Pakistan, WE CAN had begun the same year as an advocacy campaign to influence policy change on honor killings, and it took the name WE CAN End Honor Killings of Women. The organizers called Aba right after the event. They had heard about this girl from a rural area who was reading her poems in public, and they asked to publish one of them on the back cover of their magazine to recruit change makers for their campaign. And they invited me to Islamabad to join the conference to launch WE CAN and read the same poem in front of seven hundred people.

I was desperate to go, but Aba was hesitant. Composing poetry about a heavy, divisive topic and being vocal about it was different from getting on a plane to become part of a national campaign. But his love and trust had given me the confidence to be stubborn. I begged and pleaded and told him I wouldn't go back to school if I didn't do this.

He saw I was not going to relent, which was how I ended up experiencing the hustle and bustle of Karachi's Jinnah International Airport at sixteen. I had seen train stations and traditional bus stations, but never this level of activity. Once on the plane, I gripped my seat tightly and held my breath. I remembered a morning when my aunt and I sat on the floor of our kitchen hut in the *haveli* making flour *rotis* over the burning embers of cow dung patties. As I rolled the small piece of dough in my hands and put it on the *bishenk* for my aunt to throw in the fire, we heard a soft buzz in the blue sky above. We looked up to see the tiny dot of an airplane moving across the vast sky—we stared in awe.

Now I was on such a plane. It lifted off the ground. I felt as if a string were pulling on it, and if I breathed, the string would let go, and the giant pill-like machine would fall from the sky.

At the conference, activists, politicians, entrepreneurs, speakers, media groups, writers, poets, students, scholars, and even police officers were in attendance. Everyone who was passionate to end the custom of honor killing had gathered here. I couldn't believe it was happening and that I was a part of it! But my excitement turned into nausea when we were shown pictures of bloody murdered women, murders that had been reported to the police: young women, old women, sisters, mothers, wives, cousins. A sister shot in the eyes by her brother; a woman lying on the ground cold, just because she had looked out the window of her home at a strange man in the street. Emotion flooded me, and I ran outside the hall and cried as I had never cried before. When I went back inside, I felt a new clarity and resolve. I didn't care what my peers said—I knew what my path was, what journey I was beginning.

About one thousand women are killed each year in Pakistan in the name of honor. And these are just the reported cases. I was going to end this custom or die trying.

That evening I read my poem and danced to the WE CAN campaign song with Samina Peerzada, a famous national television actress and women's rights activist who has inspired thousands of Pakistani women to step into their true potential through her TV programs and other initiatives. At the end of the event, I mustered my confidence and approached the twenty kindest-looking people in the room to ask for their business cards, hoping to make connections for the future. The WE CAN campaign had disseminated information in print, on television, and on the radio. It ran in several districts across Pakistan, raising awareness of people against honor killings, doing advocacy on policy, and pressuring the government to implement policies that protected women.

CHAPTER 15

A Youth Revolution

THE NEXT DAY, BACK IN ABA'S OFFICE IN KARACHI, I spread the business cards in front of me like rare treasures and carefully typed each name out in separate emails. I sent them all the same note:

TO: *Chris Wardle*
SUBJECT: *hello*

> *Hi*
> *This is Khalida Brohi, how are you, we had some great conversations together. Hope to meet you again sometime soon.*
> *Take care*
>
> *Khalida Brohi*

It was a start to my new life. I continued my education and participated in events organized by WE CAN: workshops, rallies, protests, and focus group discussions. The main thrust of the campaign was to get the government to adopt policies that were harder on honor killings. Pakistan had accepted a number of key international commitments to gender equality and women's human rights—the Beijing Platform for Action, the Convention on the Elimination of All Forms of Discrimination Against Women, the Millennium Declaration, and the Millennium Development Goals—but none of them had brought protection to women in tribal areas of Pakistan. WE CAN pushed for the implementation of laws and raised people's awareness of honor killing.

Deeply inspired, it occurred to me that the places that most needed to hear this message—the remote tribal areas where most honor killings occur—were the places least likely to be touched unless we engaged them directly. So I wanted to bring the WE CAN campaign to my own community, to my family and friends back in my villages, where my cousins continued to be victims of honor-related crimes. I wanted to start a youth revolution in my village. I wanted to bring young voices together, strengthen them, and ready them to stand up for women's rights in tribal areas.

In Kotri, they did not receive my reaction to Khadija's murder well, and I couldn't start campaigning there. So I decided to start in Balochistan instead.

And so that summer, as my family climbed into the bus to go to Balochistan for summer vacation, I joined them, but this time I was determined to create groups of youth and empower them.

To make it happen, I knew I had to recruit my grandmother. In tribal village life, every family respects their own elders as well as the elders of other families. Bhalla Ama, my grandmother, was a respected elder. If I could get her to walk with me to the other houses, it would send a much stronger message than if I went with a cousin or an aunt. Her presence would ensure that my message was received without anger, and even if others in the village didn't immediately understand my message, it would at least get a hearing.

But my plan hit a snag: Bhalla Ama was not on board with it.

I approached her as she was sitting on a cot, where she had just taken a short nap. She was having her midmorning chai, surrounded by my four aunts and a dozen children. A few neighbors sat to the other side of the veranda on the floor, and my siblings played outside in the open.

"Why would we go to the houses of these other girls?" Bhalla Ama asked me, confused. "What are you trying to do?"

The other women echoed Bhalla Ama's skepticism. They couldn't see the wrongs in the cultural restrictions that I was trying to describe, or the physical and emotional harm some traditions inflicted on women. I did not yet understand that one debilitating effect of honor killings is that they make the women who are left behind think nothing of domestic violence, seeing it as natural and ordained.

This project was going to be harder than I thought. I had assumed my main task would be to change the minds of the men—I hadn't counted on having to change the minds of the women too. I had to frame my request in a way that would get them to listen.

I had to strategize.

From 1998 until 2002 and again in 2005, Balochistan had faced devastating droughts. Eighty percent of livestock had died, and hundreds of people perished due to malnutrition and disease. Male family members were not able to find work in the fields, and some families were so desperate for income that they went against their strict rules and allowed their daughters to look for jobs.

"Bhalla Ama," I said, "if you take me to the houses of these girls, I will Insha Allah [God willing] help them find good jobs by training them." I didn't know how exactly I was going to execute this, but I knew it was the best way forward.

AND SO, WEARING OUR long colorful veils, Bhalla Ama and I went into the small streets behind our *haveli* where some of my childhood friends still lived. Every time we knocked on a door, I held my breath, hoping the girl I had once bested in races down the street would still be there and not married off. And once we were talking, my other fear was that an uncle or father would walk in on us.

Traditional visits to other people's houses in Balochistan are very formal. As you go into a house, you are greeted silently, not with shouts or with waves but with deep hugs. Then the hosts take your right hand and kiss it. Our relatives in the mountains do this whether the guest is a girl or a boy and will often put the guest's hand on their eyes before kissing it. This is a form of giving respect to the guest and a *rehmat* (blessing) from God. The family then leads you to a special room reserved for guests called an *otaq*. Draped in beautiful hand-embroidered fabrics and tasseled tapestries, *otaqs* are filled with colorful round pillows and wool rugs. You sit on the far side of the room by the wall while they sit opposite you by the door, mostly because as a guest, you are like royalty and the hosts are your servants. Then the formal greetings begin. *How are you? How is your husband? How is your family? How is their health? How are your kids? How is their health?*

The questions slowly move from one person to another according to the order in which the conversation began. After the greeting, chai is served. You cannot rush the process, as its love and grace restore your spirits and make you feel welcome. Once the chai arrives, you approach the topic you came to discuss. During this time, I feared that the male family members would look at me suspiciously or even interrogate me. As it turned out, in only one place did the girl in the house refuse to come sit next to us. We were told that her father didn't approve of NGOs (nongovernmental organizations). The acronym was pronounced in a way that made it sound like a filthy thing.

I kept my message simple, so that girls could easily talk about it and solicit support from their families: "I am here to talk about the current inflation of prices in town," I would say, then discuss the price of flour and other staples. With the level of poverty rising, the number of jobs falling, and opportunities for work almost vanishing, inflation was the most talked-about topic among locals. I hinted that at such a time, the employment of women could benefit the whole family. I invited them to attend a group meeting. "I want us to sit together and form a union of women who can work together to bring job opportunities to one another," I told them, and asked them to bring other girls with them to the group meeting.

I recruited my maternal uncle Manzoor as an ally. He had once lived with us and gone to school with us in Hyderabad. My other uncles didn't love what I was doing, but they didn't try to stop me. They saw that my father, a man whose organization provided economic aid to their communities, supported me. Manzoor, with his good education and great manners, was able to quickly spread the message I gave the women, except tailored to men. The message was popular.

The day of the first group meeting, I swept the floor of Manzoor's mud room. I put down traditional *rilis*, dusted everything, and covered several *patis* (chests for clothes) with fabrics. The room looked colorful, bright, and full of hope. I dressed myself in the most serious, adult manner I could. I put on makeup, emphasizing my eyes, as I always feared they didn't show when I wore glasses. The only lipstick I could find was green in the tube but turned pink on my lips. Fortunately the door of the *haveli* had recently been painted with a fresh coat of cheerful blue, but the rest of the space didn't look professional at all, with cows and a few goats roaming around. One whole wall was covered with cow dung patties. A stack of wood lined one wall; every evening my grandfather chopped small pieces for the fire. Children's clothing hung on a line stretching across the *haveli*. In several places wooden poles stuck out of the ground—they held the mosquito nets every night when the cots were brought out for our beds. The room would have to do.

There was a knock at the door. My heart beat quickly, as it had the day I was told about Khadija's murder. Someone opened the door, and a girl carefully holding her chador over her face came in, led by a small boy. The presence of a boy, either young or old, is considered safe for women. Boys are taught to be guardians of women and are expected to be man-like from the age of nine, even if all they want to do is to go outside and play. It was sad to me that this girl could not come on her own without a male chaperone, but I was happy she was there anyway. I greeted every girl who came to the door with confidence, as if a huge revolution were beginning right there in our mud *haveli* in the small village in Khuzdar. It turns out, it was.

Seeing more and more girls come gave me confidence. We put the curtain down over the entrance to the room where we were gathered. My aunts brought water and tea but didn't sit with us. After the formal greetings, we began. I needed to break the ice because as I had learned from my father, sometimes the things people need to discuss the most are the things they can't bring themselves to talk about.

I looked around. Girls had taken off their chadors and put on the scarves they usually brought along in small plastic bags to visit someone. They all looked comfortable but shy. Many of these girls hadn't seen one another since childhood, maybe since arguing in the street or playing with a shared doll. It felt like a moment of freedom to speak and laugh and rejoice, yet the room was silent. Reluctantly, one girl spoke, then another. Soon they were all sharing memories, creating a portal to childhood, while I was focused on the future.

"*Masha Allah* [praise to God], look at us. Thank you so much for coming, all of you," I began, mustering all my courage. I had made a list of things I wanted to discuss, starting with the need for women to work and bring income to their families. I told them how important it was for women to help now that the drought was over.

There was silence. Someone smiled a little, but the others stared at their laps—a common gesture among women in Balochistan.

I kept going. "I want to ask you all something. Why do you think we girls haven't been outside and doing jobs? What is wrong with this idea?"

They shuffled uncomfortably. To a friend who normally loved to talk at any occasion, I said, "Come on, Robeena. I know you want to say something." A few girls giggled.

Robeena looked up and said seriously, "Yes, I don't understand that either." She fell silent.

Then a tiny, thin girl with a loud, bright voice said, "I think it's because there are so many men outside who are ready to stare you down as soon as you are in the streets. I hear some men even shout vulgar words to women."

A burst of anger passed through the room. They had all been given similar reasons as to why they were kept home. They were now talking loudly about the injustice of it all.

I asked next if they saw women as problem solvers. Most of them answered that problem solving was the job of the elders. "I think sometimes a woman would like to help the family, but they are not taken as important enough to be heard," Shahida said.

I knew what she meant. A woman chopping tomatoes in the kitchen and making dinner for eighteen people was not usually invited out to the veranda, where the men sat talking about an issue that affected them all. Very often men decided on a girl's marriage by sitting and talking in this way, without involving the women in the other room.

"How can women be powerful?" I asked. "Do you think it will mean talking in louder voices? Having an extra presence in those rooms? Or what?" The room buzzed with excitement, and the girls looked around.

"I think the elder women can be powerful because they can be heard," Robeena commented.

She was right: in our communities, age brings respect. Age isn't determined by number of years, because no one really knows when they were born. It is determined instead by the number of children one has married off and how many of those children had children of their own.

A cousin about five years younger than me was always muddy, her hair uncombed. But one summer when she came to visit, all the women got up to greet her formally. She had beautifully oiled braids, *miswak* teeth (cleaned with a tree bark), and a neat dress. She had been married off at twelve years old, so although I was older, she was treated with more respect. Women who have married off their children and are grandmothers are respected—even by men—for their wisdom.

I had to find a way to get to the most sensitive issue of all, honor killings. I asked these women what they thought about a girl being mercilessly murdered because it had been decided that she had dishonored her family.

A wave of uneasiness went around the room. Just moments before, the girls had been heatedly discussing the topic of respect for women, but there was now silence.

I understood that I had to steer the discussion back to a more manageable task. "What can we collectively do to bring strength to women? How can we help them escape customs that enforce violence upon them?"

The girls had many ideas: respecting and supporting one another in specific daily interactions; carrying ourselves more gracefully; talking to our mothers about respect; talking to our younger daughters about respect. The room was buzzing again with energy.

In the end, we all decided that women create their place in family decision making by earning respect and taking responsibility. We decided that the fight for women's rights needed to begin with getting girls out of their houses. And so gradually the youth group I had been envisioning became a reality.

On the heels of that meeting, I formed the Youth and Gender Development Program (YGDP), to educate, empower, and strengthen youth against cultural restrictions, enabling them to speak up about customs like honor killing. We would give them skills and purpose and a voice.

Aba allowed me to use his office space at PDI in Balochistan for our first meetings. My family, my friends, and I pooled our money to start skill- and job-training centers. We bought six small hand machines for a sewing center. My uncle Manzoor's friend, a local tailor, volunteered to train the women and girls. The thread and scissors were donated, and the fabrics they practiced sewing on were old banners used by Aba's organization. We also started a computer learning center, with three or four computers for both men and women. We offered English-language classes and created a lending library. We used two of Aba's rooms and split everything into two shifts, morning and afternoon. The men would come in the morning, more than thirty boys and men; girls and women came in the afternoon, eighteen to twenty of them. We had only one volunteer tutor for each group, but all the participants were hungry to learn, so they taught one another, helping one another along.

Before long, scores of youth were flocking to the door of our office. Girls and boys lined up for enrollment, and there was laughter and celebration everywhere. I would stand in a corner and watch the young beaming faces, my heart full of happiness and pride. The YGDP was self-funded, and I was still learning how to solicit donations. We started small, with just one facility in one town. That made sense to me, since I had grown up learning that you don't need money to create something with big impact—you just need big vision.

Soon we formed a cricket club, which became a way to bring greater cultural awareness to taboo issues. We brought young men together for the games, then during breaks in the play, we would engage them in group discussions about gender rights and the different opportunities that men and women had in tribal societies. Although many of the men were skeptical at first, the cricket matches became a subtly subversive way to encourage men to speak out against honor killings, exchange marriages, and child marriages. When the match got to a point where no one could leave because they were so interested in which team would win, one of our group members would broadcast a message: "Now let's talk about women's rights in Islam." This shocked many men, but nobody left. The messages from the match would spread to the market, over chai, over meals, and slowly once-taboo topics were more commonly discussed. Gradually, more men started seeing their wives, mothers, sisters, and daughters not as secret objects to be hidden away but as valuable human beings who could make important contributions.

We gave official certificates to graduates of our courses to assist them with getting jobs. The English and computer skills we provided ensured not only that more youth got hired for good jobs but also that more *women* were selected for those jobs. Usually women came in with skill levels below the men's. Until now, they'd simply had no resources to bring them up to par.

CHAPTER 16

The WAKE UP Campaign
Against Honor Killings

As the work at the YGDP was ramping up, I heard from Christopher Wardle, one of the people I had emailed after the WE CAN launch conference in Islamabad the year before. He recommended that I apply to a youth partnership program by Oxfam Australia, designed to support youth projects and ideas for global change. I had never been outside Pakistan. All I knew of the Western world were the Disney movies that my siblings and I had seen all our lives (and still eagerly watch). If I were accepted into such a program, I didn't know how my parents would take the news.

I applied anyway. While filling out the application, I felt ashamed to be writing to people in Australia about such a devastating problem as honor killings in Pakistan. It made my country look ignorant and backward, I thought, when in reality the country had so much rich culture, intelligence, beauty, and humanity to celebrate.

Sometime later I got a letter saying I was selected as an

"action partner" for the program. I read and reread it, unable to believe it: I would travel to Sydney to learn how to financially support my projects and grow them into something huge.

Life was coming to a beautiful place, it seemed. I was finally using my anger for a purpose—to change mind-sets and lives. And at the same time I was trying to concentrate on school.

As I took on the mission of applying for a visa, it dawned on me that I needed a passport. I didn't know the first thing about applying for one, or where those small photos came from, but I did understand that governments required them for international travel. But before I could get a passport, I needed an ID card. And before I could get an ID card, I needed an even more basic document: something called a birth certificate. *What does it mean to "certify" that I was born?* Aba made inquiries at a hospital, and soon enough a crisp white sheet of paper arrived stating that I was born in Hyderabad on October 10, 1988 (mistakenly choosing the same birth year as my brother's, but I finally had a birthday!). It would be a long time before we came to celebrate it, as this was a new concept for our tribe. Even today it remains a novelty.

The instructions on the application forms might as well have been in Portuguese for all the sense they made to me. Thankfully, Aba had been through much of this for his own work. After weeks of preparation, setbacks, misunderstandings, and a healthy dose of *jugar* (making things work with creative problem solving), we finally made it happen. All in all, the process took several months.

These days when I am at a conference or speaking on stage, I smile in my heart. People listening to me now have no idea what I went through to get here. I had to collect pocket money and ask my family and friends to help pay for the passport. I stood in line after line on hot days, only to be sent back home empty-handed. But how grateful I am that it all actually worked.

When the visa arrived, Ammi went from being worried to full-blown anxious. I was going to a world completely different from ours. I hadn't even made friends properly at home. All I knew was our little apartment in Karachi and our two family homes in Sindh and Balochistan. This foreign country with its white people and heavy accents was going to eat me up and destroy my values. And what would we say to our relatives? Most girls weren't allowed even to go next door, let alone to another continent, and a Western continent at that. Aba had mentioned that he would make up something if someone were to ask, like I was in the bathroom. I thought it was hilarious. Later, when I was out of the country, a cousin came to visit. Aba joked to me that he couldn't tell him I was in the bathroom because he stayed for days.

When I finally left, I sat proud and fidgety in my airplane seat next to two perky European girls. They were starting new lives in Australia, they told me, and had never been there before. I liked that all three of us in that row felt the same curiosity and excitement. The plane descended into Sydney, and one of the girls exclaimed in a thick accent, "Look! It's the opera house!" Out the window I could see a building with layer upon layer of shimmering metal roof. It looked like a flower bent down with grace. I was amazed. *So Oprah lives in this house?* It was beautiful! (Not until 2013, when I met Oprah, did I find out she didn't live there.)

During my two weeks there, Australia became my door to the wider world. I came to feel deeply connected to the activists who were part of the program. I was suddenly not alone in my struggle, and every time I spoke, I felt I had the support of hundreds of people.

I experienced many "firsts" in Sydney. It was the first time I saw people drink alcohol. It was the first time I saw couples holding hands. It was the first time I saw pubs. And it was the first time I saw dog food. (The first night I arrived, I went to buy cookies and bought dog biscuits instead. I would have never known if my friend hadn't stopped me from eating them!) It was also the first time I saw girls with real freedom. They traveled freely. They were on television. They ran companies and worked side by side with men. They were free to speak their minds and wear whatever they liked.

At first I felt disgusted by all these freedoms, and self-conscious about my traditional ways. Not until I left did I realize what my experience in Australia had really gifted me. It had poured fuel on my fire. It gave me the space to allow it to burn outside me. I wanted the freedom I saw in Australia for the women in Pakistan. My childhood friends in the village weren't allowed to laugh loudly because it was too immodest. In Sydney, women shone with confidence that reached into the hearts of those they worked with. The activists gathered there from all around the world made me believe in the connectedness of us all. I understood that thousands of people out there in the world would stand up with me, and that supporters were closer than I thought.

And so a whole new fire, determination, and courage took root in my heart. I had been cautious with the YGDP so far, touching only gently on the subject that mattered most to me. But now I was powerful and brave enough to go home and turn my initiatives into a revolution—a real fight against honor killings. I would use the Internet to connect with the people I had met in Australia and would grow something big and strong.

TWO YEARS EARLIER MY father had brought home our first computer. That huge hunk of plastic, metal, and wires upended our lives. It came from a secondhand store, in several pieces. My brother Ali spent hours attaching the wires carefully before he finally got it up and running. Then Ammi took a soft clean cloth and wiped every piece of it with a little blessing. We decided that each of the children would be allowed ten minutes to use it. I had used my father's computers at PDI's small office, but having a computer in our own house—a tiny house that flooded regularly with wastewater from the open sewers and had a curtain instead of a door—made us feel like we had moved up in the world.

The first thing I did was get on the Internet and visit the Disney website and a site for Nickelodeon cartoons. Then I started to explore more deeply. I discovered Facebook. And

I learned about Google (pronouncing it "Joogle" for a long time). Joogle was everything I wanted. What limitless power it held! Similarly Facebook, with its ability to connect people from all over the world through their pictures and mutual friends and interests, fascinated me. We kids had to use our ten minutes of allotted computer time wisely. Because I was the eldest girl, more domestic tasks were expected from me, and I was always the last to finish my chores. So when I finally washed that last dish, I would frantically dry my hands on my dress and run for the computer to get my ten minutes in before bedtime.

Coming back from Australia, I knew how I could use those ten minutes most wisely. I launched the WAKE UP Campaign Against Honor Killings. And it all started with a Facebook page. In the YGDP, I had not been able to touch upon the issue of honor killings directly because it was too sensitive and affected the communities too deeply. From my time in Sydney, I knew that so much more was possible, that we had to force the government not just to enact policies but to *implement* them. I wanted global engagement. I designed the WAKE UP campaign around a strategy of 3A's—Awareness raising, Advocacy, and Alliance building. By recruiting support throughout the world, I believed we could force government leaders to change Pakistan's policies on honor killings and implement those changes to create real protections for women.

The WAKE UP campaign's Facebook group soon had thousands of people liking and following it. I received messages of support and hundreds of comments from people. We started dialogue groups and shared posters online to spread awareness. As more people joined, we encouraged them to participate in the discussion platform and to tell three to five people about honor killings. I was persistent and sent the link to everyone I knew, urging them to join. I emphasized how important this issue was, and I shocked people with its urgency. Support came pouring in from all over the world through this portal. I joined the United Nations Population Fund as a youth adviser on sexual and reproductive health rights. I set foot in gatherings of upper-middle- and elite-class Pakistanis, among other young people who were confident, educated, and passionate to change the face of this country.

I did more research about Pakistan's laws on honor killings. I was shocked to discover that in 1977 General Zia-ul-Haq, who had become president through martial law, enforced a new set of ordinances that claimed to Islamize the 1973 constitution of Pakistan. Among these Hudud Ordinances, *qisas* (retaliation) and *diyat* (compensation) were later used the most to justify honor killings. Under *qisas* and *diyat*, a killer could be forgiven if the family of the victim forgave him. In a case of *zina* (extramarital sex), a woman who was raped had to bring four male witnesses to prove she had been raped. Otherwise she would be punished in the name of honor. It outraged me but also fueled my desire to work harder for change. Later in 2006, the Women Protection Act would be passed, strengthening the laws around honor killings, but the Hudud Ordinances would remain in effect, essentially nullifying the protections of the new law.

In Balochistan the youth groups we had formed in the

YGDP now took part in the WAKE UP campaign. The taboo on discussing this issue seemed finally to be lifting. Then amid these little steps toward a larger-than-life goal, I was selected to be a fellow at the International Youth Foundation, a nonprofit based in the United States that works to promote global youth development and empowerment. I was invited to participate in a week-long event to inaugurate this fellowship.

Although I was honored to be chosen, my first reaction to the thought of going to America was one of fear. Traveling to Australia was one thing—but going to America was another thing entirely.

CHAPTER 17

To America for the First Time

O N SEPTEMBER 11, 2001, PAKISTAN WATCHED WITH horror and sadness at the brutal attack on innocent lives. Our hearts ached with grief. Our teachers led us in prayers for the lives lost and the sorrow of their families. And then we all watched helplessly as America invaded one country after another. We all wondered if Pakistan would be next. Our young friends often scared one another with gossip about flying robots that could sneak into our villages and cities.

Now when my friends and family heard I was selected for the fellowship, they urged me not to go. Everyone warned me about what had happened to Muslims in the United States after 9/11. Girls had their scarves snatched from their heads, I was told. Bearded men were ridiculed, and kids were bullied in schools.

Ammi was especially concerned. "I'm sure they can send you your award," she said seriously. "Haven't you heard? These days they can send you things like letters but in big boxes!" According to her thinking, this was why I did not need to travel.

But my curiosity was greater than my fear, so I applied for a visa.

The process of getting a visa to go to Australia had been difficult, but I had no clue how hard it would be to get to the United States. The visa application wanted all my life details, my parents' details, my siblings' details, and my work details. With the scarcity of paperwork and documentation in Pakistan, it was an eye-opening experience for me to know how much evidence you need to prove your existence!

For the visa, I had to fly to Islamabad to be interviewed at the American embassy. Hundreds were making applications that day; we stood in a line at four A.M. to beat the crowd. The process was slow and detailed. When my turn came for the interview, my knees were shaking. Americans were going to have me: whether they were going to beat me, bully me, or just hate me, I would be at their mercy.

Little did I know that God had completely different plans for me.

My visa arrived three months later, and I was to fly to Washington, D.C., in November 2008. I had no idea that my arrival would coincide with one of the most historic moments in American history. Barack Obama had just won the presidential election, and the hotel where I was staying with the other activists was only twenty minutes from the White House. Out in the streets people held posters and banners expressing love and support for the Muslim world. Their empathy for our people beamed through the streets of Washington, and the city seemed to be glowing with a new beginning. It infused me with hope and excitement.

On the day of the election, white people with yellow hair, whom I had been scared of only the day before, cried with hope and joy for their nation. I cried too. Suddenly I was a part of their history, and that made me a part of their future. And I was proud of it. I was no longer afraid.

America, like Australia, was not what I had imagined. I had watched Disney movies my entire life with my siblings and cousins. That's how I had developed my desire for an American accent. I read about two hundred novels in English in two years, trying to become fluent. But none of the books or movies prepared me for my visit: for the strong smell of coffee, or the fact that people greeted you with a big smile, or the way they asked, "How are you?" and then turned to another customer while you were describing your current life situation. I noticed everything: the big refrigerators, the toilet seats, the piercings, the beautiful yellowing of tree leaves like a poem being told, the sky so blue and clear. I was prepared for none of it. Although my trip was for just a week, it was long enough for me to learn that humans sitting far away from one another are bound to have poor judgment about one another. I realized this is why our Prophet Muhammad P.B.U.H. advised people to travel in order to learn.

Only a week later I returned to hardships in Pakistan.

WAKE UP had organized some rallies out in the streets that were not received well. A strangeness was in the air. One day my father received a crumpled-up ball of paper saying his daughter was a threat to this community and its women. According to that letter, I was leading young girls toward Western and un-Islamic values, and I needed to beware.

This letter shook Aba. He took me aside to warn me, but I refused to be cowed. I had clearly hit a nerve, and though people were hiding behind Islam to condemn me, it was in fact Islam that condemned the behavior we were trying to change. In the United States, I had met with some of the most amazing entrepreneurs and activists from all around the world, and I felt newly empowered. These challenges seemed small in the face of that feeling.

But I had to have a sense of realism too. I started wearing the veil, covering my whole face with the long chador. But it wasn't enough.

One morning as I was riding with some of our team members to our office, we passed some young people on the side of the road throwing stones. I thought I was imagining it, but then rocks came flying at our car, popping loudly as they hit the metal and glass. Our driver had to rush through the small street.

On another morning, we arrived at the office to find the metal signs with our office name and contact information torn down, bent, and beaten as if to teach us a lesson.

Aba insisted that I return to Karachi immediately so that no real harm would come to our family or to me. At home, he took my phone from me. He demanded I shut down my Facebook and Twitter profiles and put strict rules on my coming and going out of the house, allowing me only to go out for college classes. The YGDP came to its end. The WAKE UP campaign was crushed and silenced. For the first time since I began my work, I felt utterly defeated.

CHAPTER 18

Don't Cry, Strategize

MY FATHER ONCE GAVE ME A PIECE OF ADVICE THAT would become the cornerstone of both my work life and personal life. As a child, I had a mostly cheerful nature and was quick to laugh. But I could just as quickly turn into a weeping ball of sadness, as I did each time I heard about a friend getting married off too young, or another friend being forced to stop going to school because she got her period. I cried every time I saw a mark on the faces of my aunts, the bruises from domestic violence. To weep, I hid behind curtains, put my face in a pillow, or stood behind the old metal door of our *haveli*, crying in secret.

One day I was playing with my friends in the street and asked after one of my very close friends. They told me she was no longer allowed to play with us because she was engaged to be married and her family was planning her wedding. I dropped everything and ran home. I cried and cried, and as I threw myself through the front door, my father caught me in his arms. I cried until I couldn't see through my tears.

Then, while stroking my wild hair, he whispered gently: "Shhh . . . don't cry, my daughter. *Strategize.*"

I didn't understand what he was saying at the time, but he repeated this advice whenever I cried. Only as I grew older did I begin to understand what he had been telling me: that every challenge must be met not with despair but with a plan, even if the heart is in pain.

Aba saw life as a battleground to fight for one's rights and for those who are voiceless. He fought for his own education *and* that of his daughters. As a young man, when he was writing poetry and working as an activist, he had been ridiculed, thrown out of houses, and gone hungry. "I welcomed insults," he had told me once, with deep pride lingering in his voice. "I wanted people to put me in my place, because how else was I to find my place and my path?" Every challenge cleared his vision for him, and so he learned to strategize, to give us a life that he never lived.

I promised to live by this advice; to make sure I didn't complain about problems or challenges in my work but instead devised a plan to solve them. But sometimes I still did let myself cry. Because for me, unburdening our hearts lets us see the path ahead more clearly. In 2009, I realized that I had not strategized effectively, and as a result everywhere I looked I saw failure: in people's anger at my work, in my own tribe's sadness, in my father's disappointment.

The last especially tore at my heart. Aba told me that with the WAKE UP campaign and my travel to America, I had taken the issue of honor killings too far and too public. His behavior toward me started to change. Even after taking away my phone and insisting I delete my social media accounts, he shut me out. He didn't discuss things with me anymore. Ammi kept telling me it was temporary, but I often saw her crying in the kitchen. She had never thought our father-daughter bond would be affected by anything, certainly not at the level where the whole house suffered. To this day, I am amazed by how little I understood the pain I caused my family by pushing things too far too soon.

People suddenly thought ill of my father because of the rumors about me, even in our own villages. People who had respected him for his bold decisions were shocked. And those who had told him that educating his daughters was a bad idea now shook their heads in dismay, saying, *I told you so.* His nonprofit projects in the local communities suffered as a result of his connection to me and my character. I had made a mistake somewhere, but at first I didn't realize where, or how, or even what. I certainly had no idea how to fix it.

According to Aba, my outrage at the customs in Pakistani society at the time of the WAKE UP campaign had been too blatant. I had let anger lead me and dominate discussions with young people. By launching the WAKE UP campaign, I felt I had been given permission to speak my mind and turn my rage against my culture, my people. I had not been diplomatic enough.

The more I thought about it, the clearer it became to me. I had challenged people's—*my* people's—beliefs. I had disrespected and accused people of being criminals. I had led with my emotions, and as a result, chaos ensued.

I was sad that I couldn't speak to Aba about it; he had fallen silent. His obvious disappointment in me seemed to grow. Pain now seemed to live in my heart all the time. I wondered if he wanted me and my ideas to stay small: *Is he afraid of my doing things that will really stir the air and kick-start real change?*

This prospect confused and troubled me, because this was the father who loved and adored me. This was the father who had put me on his shoulders and declared his pride for me in the village when no other fathers did such things for their daughters. He held my little hand and told me I would be an important leader someday. He had seen the strong woman in me and helped me to become her. How could he be afraid of my campaign against honor killings? Hadn't he been waiting for me to do something like this? I was his revenge for all the injustices he had witnessed and endured. I was his voice, his strength, and his little girl. . . .

That was it—I was his little girl. Like any father in this world, he wanted to keep me from harm, but my recent actions had proved that I wasn't afraid to jump right into harm's way. Acknowledging this soothed my heart and empowered me further. As the days passed in Karachi, I decided that Aba did not want me to stop doing my work, but that I needed a new strategy.

Although I had no access to my phone, I did have access to the single shared computer in our house. So when nobody was using it, I would sit at the wooden desk for hours, immersed in PDF documents, slide decks, and reports—from respectable organizations in Pakistan that had been working for women's rights for years, and from international organizations like UN Women that were advocating for the very changes I wanted to bring about. *So many of these organizations are fighting honor killings,* I noticed. *Why is so little change happening in Pakistan?* These global documents filled me with new kinds of knowledge, very different from my indigenous knowledge. I was inspired. I soon discovered what had gone wrong with our campaign. All those Google searches helped clarify the issue in my mind, but the real insight came from my own personal experiences.

One of them happened during a visit to our extended family in Kotri for Eid, on a morning when the *haveli* was full of the chaos of a big family. Some kids were still sleeping on the cot. Infants were crying, kids were playing in the courtyard, and women were picking up the beds they'd spread out the night before and sweeping. Some of the men had left to tend to their small shops and fruit carts, while others were home sipping chai and talking.

That morning, one of my aunts who had been married off in a distant village arrived with a long burqa covering her whole body, two small children in tow. Women encircled her, hugging her and kissing the children's cheeks.

That was when I saw her face. Brown and purple patches covered her skin, and there were scratches on her swollen cheeks. "My husband beat me with a broom," she explained, sadness pouring through her eyes. Many women *tsk-tsk*ed in disapproval. They asked her to take off her burqa and offered her water. There were so many sounds:

the women talking and tending to my aunt; children crying and laughing; distant men speaking and laughing loudly. But I felt as if everything stopped when her mother said, "My daughter, if you feed him and take care of him, he would never do such a thing." Women sitting and nursing their infants nodded in agreement, as if passing along a piece of wisdom that everyone except my aunt with her battered and bruised face knew.

I was confused. *Who is at fault here?* I wondered. *The woman for not feeding and caring for her husband, or the man himself, who should learn to respect the woman who gives birth to and feeds and nurtures his children in his home?* Many other times I'd heard women talking to one another after meeting with abuse or mistreatment from men: "Adi [Sister], it's our fate." "Ama [Mother], it's our fate." "Women are made to go through such trials. Have patience [*sabr*]. Remember, Allah loves patient people."

Back when I was a girl in Hyderabad, I used to go with Ammi to the neighbors' houses, where she would sit and chat with the women for hours while doing embroidery. These were the happiest, perkiest women I had ever met, able to make a joke out of anything. They loved to talk and laugh.

But usually at some point one of the women would mention a sad incident in her life and begin to cry. Soon the whole room would be weeping silently. The women would sit close together, holding one another and sobbing into their scarves. The mood, once joyful, happy, and full of song, would suddenly change to one of mourning, all because of one woman bringing up a difficult story.

It didn't make sense to me. One day as Ammi washed clothes in our yard, beating the wet ones with a stick, I asked her, "Why do the women cry together? Why so quickly and so easily?"

"Khalida, my dear," Ammi began, holding the clothes, "these women have seen pain in their lives. From birth to death, they face discrimination, at times violence, and injustice, but they never have a chance to speak. Many memories burn their hearts with pain. They have all seen so much sadness but have still tried to live happily, to serve happily as wives, sisters, and mothers." Feeling helpless and locked in a system of injustice, they take every opportunity to soothe their hearts. When one shares her pain, they all shed tears because that pain deeply resonates with all of them. They console one another through their tears and at the end remind one another to be patient. Then they go back to their embroidery and their daily lives.

By sharing that pain, the women find strength in one another and become more united. But their shared belief in their own helplessness does not allow any of them to rise above that system. And that is what has to be changed.

Sabr. Patience. Women used the word generously with one another. *Sabr* is a jewel for a woman. A woman who doesn't speak about her own mistreatment meets with good fortune in the end.

I realized that our fight for women's rights was failing because we had targeted the wrong people, in the wrong way. Too many women in Pakistan were programmed to believe that they should accept everything that happened to them as their fate. They had been taught and encouraged to practice *sabr* in the face of all misfortune and abuse, no matter how intense or horrible. They accepted violent, unethical behavior in men because they believed they should. Women encouraged one another to keep silent when they were mistreated, to keep waiting, to be patient, in the belief that one day things would be fine.

In fighting for women's rights, we had forgotten to involve the women most impacted in the change-making process. Our method of activism, to insult the cultural values of our tribes, had been wrong. So they got angry at us, defending their identities and the only world they had ever known. I felt embarrassed and ashamed at my behavior. We had to learn to talk to the tribal elders in their own language. More than anything, we had to involve the women in our cause, not just work on behalf of them. I began to brainstorm about this new approach.

One thing I knew: globalization was becoming a hot topic of discussion among the tribal cultures, even if they did not understand it as such. They could see that tribes were losing their unique identities and that everyone was beginning to look the same. Once I asked my father what globalization was. He looked at me thoughtfully and said, "It means we will all wear jeans and eat hamburgers."

At the time I didn't connect it to my work with women's rights, but now a bright beam lightened my heart, and I knew I had found a better way to tackle the issue of honor killings in Pakistan: by promoting traditions in the tribal areas. By strengthening old tribal bonds and rituals that made people feel seen and safe, we could, paradoxically, work against the ones that did the opposite. We could change the definitions of honor and dishonor: dishonor should refer to a tribal community's loss of cultural identity, when it was no longer identified as separate and sacred.

I wrote a proposal to the UN's International Fund for Agricultural Development to fund a new project. We would promote local language, music, and embroidery in every village where we worked. We would compile a tribal language book. We would collect tribal songs that were becoming endangered and make a CD of them.

And we would create a skills center where women could come to do embroidery every day. While they worked, we would teach them about their rights and also about ways to sell their products to earn an income. And in the process, they could learn how to work in peer groups and how to speak up and become leaders in their homes and communities.

The proposal was accepted: we were approved to create the new project in ten villages in Balochistan using $25,000. Aba was still not happy with me, but I was thrilled to get a second chance to do something that mattered so much to me.

But when the time came for me to travel to Balochistan to start the project, Aba wouldn't let me leave Karachi. The threats against my life were still very real and ongoing. Until the danger was resolved, he would not let me even visit my relatives in the village, let alone do work there. Seeing my disappointment, he compromised by helping me build a team in Balochistan that I could manage remotely. Although it was difficult, I trained the team from afar. Our plan was to return to the villages, sit with the tribal leaders, and ask them for forgiveness for earlier actions or initiatives that had offended them. We secretly called it our Apology Project.

When my team in Balochistan told me that our first Women's Literacy and Skills Development Center had started, I danced and laughed in our little room in Karachi. Times were finally changing. Women would now gather in safe places and speak what was in their hearts instead of telling one another to be patient in the face of violence and injustice. Voicing their fears would make them strong. I finally had a great strategy.

CHAPTER 19

Being Unreasonable

Our centers in Balochistan multiplied in such numbers that I needed to know how to manage them strategically and effectively. At one point YouthActionNet of the International Youth Foundation—the organization that had brought me to the United States—encouraged me to apply to the Unreasonable Institute. This organization offered a ten-week crash course in incubating new ideas from around the world, obtaining financial support, and learning business planning and management. It could teach me how to grow the centers, to increase their scale and replicate them.

The only requirement for admission was that the participants and their ideas had to be "unreasonable." *Finally,* I thought, *a program for me!* The word *unreasonable* had been used to describe me so many times that it had started to feel like a negative brand. But at the Unreasonable Institute, it would be celebrated!

I applied, and within a week they told me I was short-listed. The day I heard I was selected, I was shocked and excited, because I knew this experience would change my life. Finally I would learn what I desired the most—how to create a powerful movement for women in Pakistan.

The crash course would take place in Boulder, Colorado, where I and twenty other entrepreneurs from around the world would spend ten weeks learning how to run a nonprofit organization. Ammi and Aba were nervous, but it was a one-time chance for me, and I knew I had to go. I assured Aba that I would come back an expert in strategic action on sensitive issues, that I would learn to manage teams and make better decisions and avoid the mistakes of the WAKE UP campaign. This assurance helped my parents see it through my eyes. So in June 2010, I flew to Denver, where I was picked up and driven an hour northwest to Boulder.

My eyes stayed glued to the window of the car as I saw open green fields, small hills, yellow flowers, and a crisp bright sky bejeweled with clouds. In Balochistan the mountains have no green on them. Their barren rocks hold their own beauty, but this green was mesmerizing. We arrived at the Unreasonable house, which was surrounded by tall trees that whistled with the wind and had a garden in the front.

I was to share a room with two young women, one American and one Indian. Right away I decorated it with hand-embroidered sheets and pillows, colorful, flowering *rilis* from my tribe. I switched out all the plain pillowcases with Pakistani patterned ones that I pulled from my big

Young Aba and Ammi in love in Balochistan.

Aba helping Khalida to swim in the village reservoir.

Khalida with her goat in the village.

One of the few photos of Khadija with her sisters. The others were destroyed when she was murdered. Khadija is the strong and confident girl on the far right.

Grandparents in the haveli *in Balochistan where Khalida grew up.*

Khalida's immediate family.

Initial Sughar mobilization meeting of tribal women and men.

WAKE UP campaign youth assembly with policy makers.

Women going to one of the Sughar Hubs that were established in villages.

A fun girls' meeting in a Sughar Center.

Khalida with Sughar women in Pakistan.

Sughar Nomads fashion show in Karachi.

Khalida speaking at the annual meeting of the Clinton Global Initiative.

Khalida in an interview with Christiane Amanpour at Women in the World.

Khalida speaking at the MIT Media Lab during her fellowship year.

Khalida and David at their ten-day wedding celebration in Karachi.

Expressions of the family upon meeting for the first time in Venice. Khalida's mother-in-law, Mary Ellen, is on the left and Aba and Ammi are on the right.

Khalida and her parents with David in Venice after her engagement.

Khalida and David starting The Chai Spot in Sedona.

suitcases. I had even brought colorful teapots and more pillow covers as gifts.

Once the course started, I felt like a misfit. None of the other Unreasonables had decorated their rooms, but they knew so much more about business than I did. They were all such great English speakers, I couldn't keep up. Their words befuddled me—they referred to money as "capital" and used other managerial terms I didn't know. I felt lost and ashamed of calling myself an activist or entrepreneur. I was not business minded. I had no written plan, no portfolio filled with papers, no business model, no ideas for generating revenue. I had only myself and my raging fire of a heart. I was embarrassed. My decorated room seemed silly. I wanted to go home.

There were coffee-making machines and trampolines. My fellow entrepreneurs introduced me to peanut butter and jelly sandwiches, watching wide-eyed as I ate my first ever bite of this traditional American food. . . . And then there was sarcasm. Sarcasm isn't a thing where I'm from. I believe almost anything I'm told.

At mealtimes, while the other entrepreneurs sat sketching important-looking diagrams and graphs, I sat alone at a table, miserable. Then Daniel Epstein, one of the institute's cofounders, came over to me. With a huge smile, he whispered, "Khalida. Tea? You and me, later today?" I felt so shy, I could only squeak a small yes.

Later, while Daniel and I sat drinking tea, he asked how I liked the classes. I blurted out everything to him. By opening up about my insecurities, I started down a whole new path with Daniel and the other Unreasonable founders. They took time to help me separately with my idea. They went out of their way to make sure I progressed along with the other entrepreneurs and did not feel left behind or inadequate. Soon I was fitting in in my own way. I began to make friends and embrace new experiences. I drank coffee without making a sour face (but with lots of cream and sugar). I ate biscuits with ice cream in the middle. I learned the electric slide. I learned not to use toilet paper for drying my hands. Most important, I learned about scale, about taking your ideas from one place to another by making them sustainable, and about mobilizing forces toward your vision.

At the Unreasonable Institute, I thought about how I had made Aba suffer through my unrealistic goals, by pushing my agenda so quickly. I felt like we had become strangers. I missed being his Khali. So that night I wrote him a long email, thanking him for everything he had done for me. I told him that I was working on media strategies, weighing risks and assumptions of security, all while learning how to play volleyball and ultimate Ping-Pong, go hiking, and throw a Frisbee. I told him that when I returned home, I would do everything in my power to create the best programs for women. And I would.

CHAPTER 20

The Stroke

I RETURNED HOME DEEPLY INSPIRED AND READY TO take on the world. But I found that while I was gone, huge monsoon rains had flooded most of Sindh Province, including Karachi, putting it under water. It affected about twenty million people, forcing thousands to migrate, while others lived in desperate conditions. I was shocked because while I was in America, I had heard no news about the floods at all. All I had seen on television were reports of local bombings and shootings.

This was more disastrous news: one of my cousins, Khadija's sister Sajda, had left home with a boy she had fallen in love with and was in hiding, fearing for her life. Khadija's murder, as happens with many honor killings, had cast doubt on the integrity of the family's remaining unwed girls. To hedge the family's honor, Uncle Liaqat had betrothed Sajda to a man in a distant village. So when Liaqat found out about her escape, he sent people to kill her wherever and whenever they found her.

Back in Boulder, I had wondered why my father never responded to my heartfelt email. Now I knew. He had been in Kotri trying to talk sense into his brother.

Ammi was the one to break the news about Sajda to me. She watched me carefully as she told me how my younger cousin, whom I had patted on the head as we played years ago, was now hiding from her own uncle, God knew where.

"They can't kill her!" I shouted as soon as she finished. *"Allah! Ammi, they can't kill her!"* My lips were dry, and my heart was barely beating. I felt selfish for feeling hurt that Aba had not responded to my heartfelt note. In fact he had been chasing his brother around, trying to convince him to spare the life of his niece. Ammi tried to console me, while in the background the television broadcast news of the floods wreaking havoc and devastation all over the province.

Families were living on roadsides, and children were dirty and thirsty and suffering. I put my own projects aside and joined Aba and his team in the rescue and relief activities. For five months, we lived in a rented house in Shikarpur, hiring sixty people to assist with relief and rescue. To seek help from the world, I started blogging, a skill I had strengthened at the Unreasonable Institute; now I used it to write stories about people who needed help. Soon people emailed me asking how they could contribute. The power and speed of the Internet amazed me! In five months, working seventeen-hour days and rarely getting more than four hours of sleep a night, we were able to help some thirty thousand people. Although I felt extremely useful to my people during that time in Shikarpur, Sajda and my other women were never far from my thoughts. I felt acutely that my other plans were going unfulfilled.

Right before the New Year, we came back to Karachi. I ached to find Sajda, to know how she was doing—and even if she was still alive. The men my uncle sent had not been able to find her, but that barely made me feel better. Her situation was unbelievable. Everyone in our tribe thought she was a criminal, even though she'd been promised to a man much older than her, to live in a village where she would have had barely enough to eat, let alone that she was in love with someone else. My father had tried to help but failed, so my chances of finding her were slim.

My heart burned with a sense of helplessness—a foreign feeling that I refused to tolerate. The devastation and poverty that I had just witnessed from the floods made me even more anxious to right such injustices. One positive thing had come out of the flood experience: more villages had become willing to let us in and to work with our projects. I was determined to make income-generating ideas a big part of the projects so that rural communities would be better able to sustain themselves. Once these opportunities were in place, the men would allow us to work more with their women, which meant that we would be able to help prevent more situations like Sajda's.

On New Year's Day 2011, I arrived home from a powerful meeting with my team reflecting on the past year and planning our year ahead. Everything was normal: Ammi had guests in our *otaq* (the room where we entertained guests), while children were reading, coloring, and watching TV in the living room. I felt a strange sensation on my pinky finger. It burned as if it were on fire. The pain radiated to my palm, then to my elbow, and soon my whole arm felt consumed in flames. Sounds became distorted, much louder, and smells were sharper. I rushed to where Ammi was sitting with guests and said, "Ammi, Ammi, I'm—"

The burning sensation reached the back of my head where it stabbed me with a final blow. I lost consciousness and seized.

When I came to, the whole family was huddled over me. Fatima cradled my head in her arm, trying to feed me orange juice through a straw. The guests had tears in their eyes, chanting verses from the Holy Quran and blowing on me so their prayers could enter my heart. Ammi was wailing with more tears than I had ever seen. Ali, also teary-eyed, was calling, "Khalo, Khalo!" (his loving nickname for me). And my younger siblings were in shock, their faces pale and frozen.

I thought I was dying. I started crying too and tried to raise my head, but—nothing. It did not budge, despite my command. My body felt like it was falling into a well, just falling and falling. I must have passed out, because when I woke again, I was in a hospital bed, in a gown with wires running down my chest. The doctors spoke hurriedly. Ammi, still weeping, stood next to me, as everyone else peeked in from the door. My family thought I had had a heart attack, so they had brought me to a cardiologist at a small local hospital. He had done an EKG, which turned out to be normal. But the blood tests revealed that I was dangerously anemic, with a hemoglobin level of 5.3. (Between 10 and 12 was normal for our women.) I needed an immediate blood transfusion, but the hospital did not have the resources to do it. I would have to be taken to a larger hospital, and my family would have to find volunteers to give blood.

No sooner had our community in Karachi found out I needed blood than men arrived in a large open-top truck, all big guys, competing for the honor to donate their blood for me. As they put an IV line into my arm and gave me all the injections necessary to start the transfer of fresh blood, Ammi stopped me from looking. I never knew I was so loved.

It turned out that I had had a stroke. The doctors discovered a blood clot on the right side of my brain. Strangely, the blood clot looked old, very old, as if it had been there since my childhood. My extreme anemia, exhaustion, and stress had somehow aggravated it. My entire left side was paralyzed, from head to toe, and I was diagnosed with seizures. The doctors advised me to stay away from bright lights, loud sounds, and emotional stress. They gave me an antiseizure medication but had no prognosis for how long the paralysis would last or even if it would pass. The whole family was terrified.

Within a week, I had another seizure. People poured in from Balochistan bringing prayer water. Some prayed on *mate* (white clay that pregnant villagers eat). Once again everyone thought that I was on my deathbed. But as when I was an infant, indigenous wisdom saved my life. My uncle,

a tribal leader in Balochistan, said I needed to do a traditional *dakh rakh*. This was an indigenous form of healing,
where I would stay in a dark, soundless room, away from
contact with any person, for forty days.

I spent forty days in seclusion. During that time, I was
administered traditional treatments and prayers. A long
red prayer string was tied around me. I heard my family
outside the dark room's thin walls, their voices fearful and
full of sorrow. I heard my brother Ali sob—I had never
heard him cry before. But whenever anyone came into the
room to feed me or take me to the bathroom or treat me,
they acted as if all were well. Part of the tribal healing process is to make the patient feel unburdened by heavy emotions.

When the forty days were over, my family members
lined both sides of the door, and as tradition required, they
raised their arms and locked their hands to create a tunnel.
I emerged from the room and walked through the tunnel
and into my restored life as a healthy person. My uncle's
prescription had worked. I regained control of my body,
though I still experienced tremors. I had been granted another shot at life, and I intended to use it to do what was
right.

CHAPTER 21

My Strategy to End
Honor Killings

FACING THE POSSIBILITY OF MY LIFE ENDING HUMBLED
me and fueled the urgency and importance of what I was
trying to achieve. I made three decisions:

1. I would do all I could to scale the idea that had
so successfully worked in Balochistan, even if it
meant focusing only on the issue of honor killings
and creating the best solutions for it.
2. My message about unleashing the potential in
women had to reach a wider audience. I would say
yes to all the media interview requests and invitations
to speak that had been piling up for more than a year.
3. I would bring Khadija's other sister, Kalsoom,
and her two youngest siblings to Karachi, even if
that meant speaking to my uncle Liaqat.

I told Aba I needed to leave the other projects I was
working on with him so I could focus exclusively on my

strategy to end honor killings. I would create a platform, however small, for women only and fulfill my promise to end this barbaric practice and give all women a chance to live full and productive lives.

Our previous approach to ending honor killings had been to target women as victims, seeking only to rescue them. But achieving our goal would take more than changing laws or men's behavior. Women's mind-sets were also part of the problem. If women earned income, gained confidence, and knew of their rights and freedoms in Islam, their status and self-esteem would rise, allowing them to live according to their wishes.

I would take the Women's Literacy and Skills Development Centers that we had established in Balochistan to the next level, calling them Sughar Centers. I chose the name Sughar because it embodied everything I wanted to see in women—skills and confidence. The word is not used a lot, but every time a woman is called *sughar,* she beams for months. I had seen it in my mother. I had felt it in myself. At the Sughar Centers, we would remind tribal women of their strengths instead of declaring their disempowerment.

We would use embroidery as a way to spread education and promote traditions, while keeping the men engaged through cricket matches and monthly gatherings. Here women could receive six months of training in skills development and entrepreneurship using traditional embroidery. We would help them refine their existing skills, then give them the tools and outlets to sell their handiwork. We would also educate them about their rights under Islam, such as their right to education, and the right to equal legal standing with their husbands, including the right to seek a divorce. The goal was to help them become leaders in their own homes, in their lives, and in their communities by unleashing their potential.

I asked Ali, who was now running a successful filmmaking company in Pakistan, to help me launch the Sughar Empowerment Society, a nonprofit organization. To make it official, I had to spend weeks gathering documentation, filling out paperwork, bugging uninterested government officials, and waiting in all kinds of lines to submit applications. Aba saw how troubled I was by the whole process and allowed me to use PDI's platform to start my initiative. Despite my trembling left arm and my limping walk, I launched the Sughar Women Program within PDI.

We proposed a partnership with the International Labour Organization (ILO), and in June 2011, the project was approved. Using thirty trainers, our project would reach three hundred women in ten villages. Time was scarce, I felt, and we needed to act fast with a lot of women. So after the successful project in Balochistan, we began to scale our work into Sindh.

I would have to hire and manage a large team of people on my own. I faced many challenges along the way, including losing my most beloved deputy to Stage 4 throat cancer. She hadn't told any of us about her illness, throwing herself into the work without restraint. We only found out when, one day, she didn't show up for work—she had passed away. Replacing her was a very emotional experience, but in the end, I hired a girl named Amina, from the town of Sukkur in upper Sindh. Amina had barely escaped an honor killing herself, for riding on a motorcycle behind a male cousin and putting her hand on his shoulder for balance. Her own brother was supposed to murder her in the name of honor. Her husband had saved her but had kicked her out of their house, saying she was unclean for him. Amina would become the heart of our organization. She would laugh so much she would cry, and she expressed joy and sadness in a big way. When she spoke, it was as if my own passion for this work were speaking through her.

Our Sughar Centers did well in the villages, and I finally felt I was getting traction with my goals. Then one day a rumor broke out in one of the villages in the Thatta district of Sindh that Sughar was teaching women Western thoughts and beliefs. Men noticed that their wives were laughing and talking loudly and even expressing independent ideas. Disapproving, some of them refused to let their wives and sisters and mothers come to the center anymore. Amina and I went to the village to fix the situation, to talk to the men. But we faced extreme opposition.

As usual, our driver parked the car far outside the village, to maximize privacy for the families. Amina and I got out, and as we walked toward the houses, I received a call from the driver. I looked back and could see him surrounded by several angry men. "Please come back quickly, Adi!" he shouted. "They are threatening to shoot us!" It was shocking but not surprising. In another village, men waved large axes to try to chase us away. Amina and I went into the village anyway. The women begged us to leave, saying we all would be harmed if we stayed.

That's when we realized we had to come up with a new plan, one that could bring women back to the center without putting them in danger.

CHAPTER 22

Pakistan's Tribal Fashion Brand

AMINA AND I MADE A BOLD DECISION TO TAKE THE embroidery products that our women were making and try to sell them in Pakistan's fashion industry. Up until that point, our women had been selling them in small exhibitions that we hosted around the country. But that was not enough. If we could increase our sales and raise our prices, the women would earn more income and could help their families on a larger scale, which we believed would change men's attitudes.

People told Amina and me that we were fools to get into such a complex industry, but I knew the women we worked with were true artisans and simply needed a platform for their work. Pakistan was on the fashion map, its models working all over the world and designers selling products globally. Pakistani designers even used patterns from indigenous communities, borrowing heavily from traditional designs. But in all our research, we came across few fashion brands that were owned by tribal women. We decided Pakistan needed a tribal women's fashion brand that would benefit and represent indigenous women while being fashionable and accessible to mainstream consumption. Amina and I were the perfect people to launch it. We would take the women's products to designers, models, and experts at high-end brands. We envisioned working with ethical fashion companies

But as we stared at photos of models with the most intricate dresses, the highest heels, and serious faces, we felt fully naïve. My own tribal dress—the traditional pocket dress—was beautiful but not trendy, and Amina simply wore whatever she found in the house. I knew that in order to be taken seriously in this mission, we had to spiff up our attire. First we slipped on some high heels, which was easy. (There is a joke that Balochistani women can climb mountains in heels. We wear them everywhere, even in the dirt and gravel.) The diva look was very fashionable, so we wore dark-colored dresses. Amina bought "cut-piece" fabrics, or remainders of beautiful chiffons, velvets, and silks, for cheap, then had them sewn for our meetings. She started wearing her hair in a puff, which looked sleek and modern. Now we could pass for fashionistas!

We met with industry experts, pretending to know what we were talking about. They drove or were driven in fancy cars to meet us, while we took rusted rickshaws (*tuk tuks*), praying that our hairdos didn't come entirely undone en route.

We chose the name Nomads because many of the women's designs were based on stories from nomadic tribes, passed down through generations. I reached out to a college friend who had become a great fashion designer, and together we planned a fashion show in Karachi. We launched Nomads in February 2012 to great fanfare, with a glitzy runway show. There the tribal women got to see models walking in their handmade creations, and we received international press coverage.

We managed to persuade an elite mall to give us a free space to set up our shop. It was in a brightly lit Western-style mall, so different from the small markets in Karachi where Ammi and I had shopped for groceries and clothes, where the vendors shout and you are expected to bargain. Now, as we stepped into that mirrored mall, I wondered if my shoes would slip on the slick floors. We walked down gleaming hallways lined with shops of international brands and food courts with Dunkin' Donuts, McDonald's, and KFC.

But the mall management wanted to be part of the change we were trying to make. We couldn't believe it when they handed us the keys to twelve hundred square feet of glass-walled prime retail space. Here was proof that confidence and self-belief have tremendous power, are even the most important factor in accomplishing anything. Here we were, a handful of indigenous village girls, opening our own high-end shop in one of Karachi's most exclusive malls.

Often entrepreneurs get stuck thinking and worrying about the cost of activities, the plans and budgets they put together. But when you take a step toward a goal with the unshakable belief that it will be successful, opportunities sometimes manifest in other ways.

We launched an e-commerce site for Nomads, then realized we needed good pictures of people wearing our products. We put out a call for models on Facebook and shamelessly made it clear that the winning model would receive only fame, because although we were convinced that this project would be the next big thing, we had no money. An incredible girl with a beautiful smile and a big heart flew all the way from Lahore just to help us, and a photographer from a local newspaper volunteered to take the photos.

ONE MORNING THE FOLLOWING WEEK, I was preparing to lead a staff meeting to discuss the next steps on what seemed like the path to exponential growth for Nomads, when Amina walked in. She told me that her husband who had once kicked her out of his house had come to get her. His mother was dying and wanted grandchildren. So even though he had thrown her out in disgrace, he had decided to take her back and start a family. She agreed to go with him.

I was stunned. I told her she couldn't go, that it was a trap, that she should seek a divorce, that she wouldn't be safe with him.

"I will go back with my husband," she said, emphasizing the word *husband*. "Adi, this has made my whole family happy." For the first time the calm on her face irritated me, and I wanted to take her by the shoulders and shout at her.

"I can't talk about this right now. You are not going, and that's that," I said to end the conversation.

This young woman had become a leader whom people listened to and admired. She spoke to reporters, sang joyful songs, and cried with happiness at even our smallest success. She had become a *sughar* woman through and through: holding her head high, feeling proud of what she was doing and what she would do next to fulfill her potential. I was afraid to let her walk back to a life of fear and violence. *How can she sacrifice her potential for a man's wish? Especially the one who threw her away?* I couldn't let her sacrifice herself. If she met the same fate as Khadija, I would never forgive myself.

To my horror, by June 2012 her decision was final: she was going back with her husband. Like a woman in a village, she would submit herself for the happiness of her family. I raged like a madwoman. I talked to attorneys about her divorce, praying that she would have some sense. Every day I went to the office only to plead with her to change her mind.

My father got angry with me for interfering in someone else's life so intimately. Calling attorneys to intervene when she didn't want it was going several steps too far, he said. For the second time, he lost trust in me. "Who do you think you are?" he asked. "Someone wants to go back to their husband, and you want to stop them?" He told me I was being unreasonable and selfish and too emotional. But what I couldn't make him understand then, and still struggle to make him understand even now, was that without my emotions, I wouldn't be doing any of this work. And that it was my unreasonableness that got things done.

In July I received an award for entrepreneurship from

the Women Development Department in Sindh, Pakistan, alongside Malala Yousafzai. During the award ceremony, I got a call: Amina had left. In a dreamlike state, I walked up to the bathroom at the venue, sat down on the floor, and sobbed into my knees. I felt tired and defeated. I had just received an award for being a woman leader, I had spent time with Malala, I felt inspired and successful, yet all the while my own team member was sacrificing her life for a man's wish. I cried for Amina, for Khadija, and for every woman I had been unable to save. Later that night, my heart still aching with sorrow, I called Aba. I wanted to hear some words of consolation and encouragement from him. But instead I just heard sternness. He ordered me to think rationally, to find some practicality in my world of dreams.

Amina was gone, and so was my father's trust in me. At the same moment, my cousin Kalsoom called to say that she and her siblings were ready to move to Karachi.

CHAPTER 23

Kalsoom

Kalsoom had become an adult at the age of twelve, on the day she sat with her sister in that dark room of the *haveli* in Kotri, unable to save her from her fate. The events that followed made her tough and unbreakable. Soon after Khadija's murder, their mother, unable to bear the sadness, passed away. Kalsoom's father died shortly thereafter, leaving her and her two younger siblings alone in the world. Then Uncle Liaqat arrived and took the children under his wing. He saw no irony in the fact that he was the reason they had lost their family and needed a new father at all. To him, this was all part of upholding the honor of the family.

Every time I thought about it, my chest filled with sadness for these children. Every single day, they had to see the face of the man who had destroyed their lives. But when I made that promise to bring the three to Karachi, I knew I had to include my uncle too, whether I liked it or not.

I had to be very clever about it. After all, I was talking about changing a lifestyle that his family had participated in for hundreds of years. I remember that first conversation I had with Uncle Liaqat. He had developed a certain pain in his abdomen that would send him sprawling on the floor for hours. He had visited doctors, taken medicines, received injections to fight the pain, but nothing helped. I told him that he had to come to Karachi to find better doctors than those in Kotri so he could recover fully. And I offered to pay for it.

My second step was to convince him to bring Kalsoom to Karachi too. She could cook the foods he needed to eat, I said, since my mother was already cooking for us eight children, and he needed a special diet. Kalsoom knew how to be a nurse and had taken on the role of caring for him, so he liked the idea. He agreed to bring her with him for an extended stay in Karachi. That opened the door for me to discuss their moving permanently. "I will give Kalsoom a job at Sughar. I have a position for her," I told Uncle Liaqat. "The children would go to better schools here, and I will find a house to rent."

During all these calls and conversations, Aba had shown concern and disapproval about what I was doing. This time I understood why. Aba had run away from the village, come to a world with fewer restrictions, started at the bottom and worked hard. Only by making these difficult decisions had his daughters been able to prosper. Now here I was threatening it all by bringing the one person who had authority over him, the only person who could give him an order that he would have to obey.

But I had to do it for Kalsoom, for her siblings, and for Khadija.

The day of the move, I sent a jeep to Kotri to help them move their stuff from the mud *haveli*. Even though I was excited for Kalsoom, my heart ached. That *haveli* was where we had played, where I had memories of Khadija, where early in the mornings the delicious smell of chai made on coal and *parathas* with traditional *ghee* wafted in the air, where we slept on cots outside in the yard. Life had changed so much. Everything in that house was gone, but the memories stayed, mocking us all.

The jeep brought their few belongings to the little apartment I had rented close to our house in the Gizri neighborhood. Later that day I went to greet them. I took the broken stairs up to the second floor. There were no lights, and the building was dark and humid, but it was a good start. Inside the apartment were small sacks with clothes and books strewn across the floor. Kalsoom was standing with her hands on her hips as Uncle Liaqat balanced on a tiny stool, fitting a ceiling fan to the ceiling, sweat dripping from his forehead. In her overwhelmingly stressful life, Kalsoom had put on weight, but she was plainly happy to be in Karachi. They had left a large *haveli*, with plenty of sunshine and breezes, for this tiny hotbox that had two holes for windows near the roof. But one must sometimes sacrifice one thing for another.

I stepped inside in my ironed cotton dress and simple *chappals* (sandals), hair tied back, and hugged her. I asked how they were doing, if they needed anything. The little ones looked grateful, hopeful, and shy. Gazing up at where

Uncle Liaqat stood on the stool, his shoulders and under-arms sticky with sweat, his eyes fixed on the fan, I felt deep pride. Life was changing for the better, right before my eyes. Things were going to be different now. My cousins now would have a shot at happiness.

CHAPTER 24

Noreen

SEPTEMBER WAS WHEN THE MONSOONS FINISHED OPEN-
ing the drains of the old city of Karachi, and the sky began
to darken quickly. It felt like a joyful time. Our work in the
villages was thriving, and although I hadn't heard from
Amina, Sughar was becoming successful, and news of it
was spreading around the world.

One day, after delivering some products to our store in
the mall, I stepped into a fully packed restroom where girls
were fixing their hair and putting on lipstick to go to a
movie on the mall's third floor. A group of them were
laughing and pointing at something. A thin girl in a black
burqa was crouching in a corner, her face turned up and
her mouth open as if she were sleeping. I shook my head
disapprovingly at the young girls making fun of this poor
soul. I went over to straighten her head so she wouldn't
wake up with a sore neck—and realized she wasn't sleeping. She was unconscious. I tried to wake her up, but she
wouldn't budge. I called for Fauzia and Hina, my younger

sister and her friend who helped us in Nomads. We splashed water on the girl's face.

Her lifeless eyes looked blankly at us as she told us to let her be.

"I can't let you be like this," I told her. "Where are you from? You probably need the hospital. *We want to help you.*"

"You can't," she finally replied.

My sister Fatima, who often helped us with communications at Sughar, brought her some juices. We continued to ask her questions as she lay there. She was reluctant to tell us anything, but eventually she divulged that her name was Noreen, that she had left her home and did not want to go back. No matter how many times we offered to help, she told us to leave her alone. I took her phone number and gave her my card.

At home that evening, I called Zehra, a Pakistani friend whom I'd met at the Unreasonable Institute. Zehra, through her incredible insight and wisdom, had stolen my heart and become a true friend forever. She was now one of the most highly networked and powerful women in Pakistan and always leveraged her connections to do good for others.

"Hello," her kind voice said, calming my nerves.

I told her about Noreen and requested help in finding a shelter for her. I sensed my siblings in the other room, silent, listening in, and my father eying me, wondering what I was up to now. He had seen me do so many outrageous things, and I could sense his frustration as he flipped mindlessly through TV stations after a long day at the office.

Zehra gave me the phone numbers of several shelters,

and soon I was calling them, pleading for help. The shelters wouldn't send a vehicle to get someone, they told me. I would have to bring Noreen in myself.

As I hung up, Aba asked carefully, "What's going on?" His voice was irritated and stern yet he could see my worried face. I told him about Noreen, and he became livid. "It's none of your business, Khalida! Do you understand these things can be political or tribal, and you could get us all in a lot of trouble?!"

I realized that although my family had risen—with great hardship—to the lower middle class, I was potentially endangering them all by inserting myself into a tribal or family feud that could turn against us. If the issue was tribal, and if the girl came from a rich and powerful family, I was seriously endangering my life and my family's.

I called Noreen and sadly gave her the number of a shelter, instructed her to get a cab, and called the shelter to let them know she was coming.

That night I heard Aba speak to Ammi before bed, a mix of disgust and disappointment in his voice. "Who does she think she is? She thinks she has hundreds of leaders backing her, all these people who cheer for her on the Internet. But none of them will come to save her if someone tries to kill her tomorrow." Ammi listened quietly, and so did I. My heart sank. The pain, the shame, and the hurt in Aba's voice were like stabs of a knife. At that moment I wished I were married. Things would be so different if I had a husband who allowed me to do what I thought was right.

I tossed and turned that night, the sad eyes of Noreen

and the angry eyes of my father in my mind. I finally dozed off around three or later, but then my phone rang. I saw Noreen's number. My heart pounded. "Hello," I said weakly.

"This is the police," a voice boomed from Noreen's phone. "This woman says she knows you, and she's refusing to give us any information. You need to get down here this minute."

My heart seemed to lose its place in my chest. It fluttered around in my whole body until I felt faint. If Aba found out about this call, everything I wanted to do for women would suffer. *Oh God, please help me,* I pleaded. *You have helped me in everything. Please guide me now. What am I to do?* I was a twenty-two-year-old girl from Balochistan. My family still struggled to overcome poverty and educate their children. My father's circles kept questioning him about his daughter's behavior and why he sent all his daughters to good schools when everyone in the tribe knew that respect and opportunities were for boys, not for girls.

And at the same time, in the midst of all his sacrifices, I had chased the dream of becoming an activist, not a doctor as he had wished. I had let myself be drawn to other people's issues, to help others when I was the one who needed help, when our family needed help as much as anyone else did. Aba was right, one political blow would destroy what he had struggled to create for us—a little house, good schooling, and a life of hope and dreams to become somebodies.

For the first time I thought that in order to be an effective activist I would have to be rich, like many other activists I had met at conferences. They came from big bungalows, not tiny old flats and mud houses. Some had uncles who were police officers. Some had relatives who were lawyers. Their aunts ran businesses. They would be protected if something went wrong. They had a safety net that allowed them to take important risks. I had no power. My uncles lived on tops of mountains and drove fruit carts in villages. No one in my family could save me. And my actions constantly put them at risk.

Tears of defeat and frustration welled in my eyes. I remembered the time when Ali and I had sold pieces of wooden crates to fruit vendors in the market to bring home some money for that day's meal. We were little children, but still Ali had felt embarrassed. I had seen the shame of poverty and the feeling of helplessness rise up on his face as the vendor handed us a few rupees in exchange. Now that shame lived on *my* face. I hated *my* helplessness and my whole being.

And I hated myself in that next moment, when I whispered to the police officer on the other end of the line, "Sorry wrong number," and turned off my phone.

I live with the shame of that moment to this day.

CHAPTER 25

The Year of Hardships

I COULDN'T LIVE IN KARACHI ANY LONGER. I HAD EX-
perienced too much stress recently and wanted to go somewhere comforting and far away and get some quiet time to
recalibrate. I decided to go to Balochistan for a few days to
check on our centers' work. I loved my mountains and my
people in Balochistan. They were my identity. Every time I
left, I missed the place more. As the rental car rolled past
the thunderous cliffs, valleys with tiny mud homes, small
schools, children laughing and playing in the dirt, women
fetching water, men working in fields, I kept wondering
how to make things right with Aba.

While I was in Balochistan, I spent my days in the office.
One evening I was typing on my laptop, responding to
emails. The rest of the team had left around five, but the
social mobilizer and the project manager were briefing me
about a recent success story in one of the villages, where
the tribal leader had invited the whole team for dinner,
happily celebrating our efforts.

Around eight-thirty the phone rang. At the *haveli*, my aunts had started dinner and were waiting for me. I often stayed at work until nine or later, but I felt guilty about making them wait, so I quickly packed up my stuff. The three of us walked out. I got in the car, waved to them, and the driver pulled away.

We had just turned onto a small road lined with small mud houses when I heard a loud thud. I thought nothing of it until we pulled up at the *haveli*. A boy frantically rode up behind us on a bike, threw it down, and ran toward us out of breath. "Office has been attacked!" he said to me. A small crowd gathered, and I learned that the sound I had heard driving away was the explosion of a bomb.

It had exploded mere minutes after we left, not only destroying the office and one of our vehicles but injuring our security guard, who was rushed to the hospital. The bomb had been intended to hurt me. The bomber had failed only because I happened to leave early that day.

This news brought the same hollow sadness to my heart that I had felt when I heard the news of Benazir Bhutto's assassination in 2007. Not only had we lost an incredible woman leader that day, but many of the young girls who dreamed of becoming the next Benazir Bhutto were now going to be afraid. On the day the bomb destroyed our office, almost killing me and my team, I knew that many other initiatives would cease because of this news.

I wasn't hungry anymore. I returned to Karachi right away.

In all my worry about what would happen next, I had not imagined the rage Aba would show me, and his fear.

"You could have been killed, Khalida! And before that you almost died of a stroke!" he bellowed. "Your doctor told me to stop you from putting your health in danger any further, but you begged me, and so I didn't stop you from your work. But then you went crazy and started rescuing people off the roads, getting into messes, creating messes, bringing my brother—who was the reason I left home—right next door to me! Why, Khalida? I ask you, why have you started this enmity with me?" The pain in his voice made my eyes blurry with tears. My whole body shook with guilt, embarrassment, and shame.

That night, back in Karachi, the pain between my father and me became impossible to contain. We had reached the point where we could no longer be under the same roof. And as if to read my thoughts, later that night, while my family pretended to sleep, he asked me:

"You must choose, Khalida, between me and this work. Which do you choose?"

The taxi arrived at two-thirty A.M. Filled with sweat and sadness, I dragged my bag down the stairs. The sound woke the watchman, who instantly came up to help me. I got into the taxi, the tears soaking my neck, my hair a mess, and my dress wrinkled. That night I was leaving everything behind.

I boarded a flight to San Francisco. When I arrived, with my mascara smeared and my hair disheveled, I was heavily interrogated by the Department of Homeland Security. My documents were jumbled, and I didn't know how to answer their questions. I was confused. It was as if I had no words. I had come to the United States without a plan, hoping to meet with entrepreneurs and mentors and speak wherever people would listen.

Later that month Sharmeen Obaid-Chinoy (now a two-time Academy Award–winning documentary filmmaker), a beautiful and strong woman, personally invited me to speak with her at Google Zeitgeist in Phoenix, a conference that brings world leaders together. I stayed in a room that was bigger than our entire house in Karachi. On the first day of the event, I met Megan Smith, another incredible woman, a powerful leader, disruptively brilliant, and deeply driven. Until my last day in Phoenix, I didn't realize that among her many roles was vice president of new business at Google. Megan introduced me to many people, including Joi Ito, the director of a place called the MIT Media Lab. Joi invited me to come to the Media Lab and share my experiences and ideas with students.

So later that November I flew to Boston to visit MIT. I didn't know what I was in for until I stepped through the huge glass doors of the Media Lab and onto its shiny marble floors. The way the students spoke to one another, the large machines, the gorgeous hallways full of scientific books—instantly I was self-conscious. The mud walls of my *haveli*, the tall mountains of Balochistan, were many worlds away.

At MIT, I spoke to people about my experiences and about the need for the women of Sughar to have access to affordable technology solutions. Whenever I Skyped with my family, my father immediately left the room. Now, as I walked through the streets of Cambridge, as I met with students and professors, I again heard his words—that he regretted giving me my freedom.

If relations with my father were going to be broken anyway, I decided that I was going to do something dramatic that would deliberately upset him. I would take a Greyhound bus across the United States on my own, with no particular place to go, simply to meet people. This *had* to be the most rebellious thing I could ever do.

I had traveled by Greyhound once before, and it had been an exhilarating experience. Greyhound was nothing like the Jhalwan Express buses we had taken to Balochistan, which had jingle bells attached to the front, were painted in bright red, orange, yellow, and blue, had lights circling like Christmas decorations, and played Bollywood songs all through the night. I rode by bus from Boston to Boulder, then went on to Salt Lake City, Los Angeles, and Phoenix, passing through at least thirteen states on my trip. I met all kinds of people: in the bus, on the seat next to me, at the stations, and on the streets. I met people who lived in poverty, people who didn't have jobs, and people who had left their small towns for cities where they tried to make a new life for themselves, as my family had done. I tasted a green paste called guacamole. I was offered my first cigarette—and politely refused. I heard stories about abortion and its laws. I talked to all kinds of women on those buses who, like me, were trying to figure out their lives. On New Year's Eve 2012, on a desolate road in Utah, I blasted Bollywood music from my phone, and bus passengers danced in the aisles.

My Greyhound trip opened my eyes to the reality that every country has its struggles, that the hardships Pakistanis face aren't unique to our society—they exist everywhere, even in America. I discovered how diverse and beautiful America is. Only then, when my heart was open to joy again, was I prepared for what God planned for me next.

CHAPTER 26

Love in Los Angeles

In THE FIRST WEEK OF 2013, MY GREYHOUND TRIP landed me in Los Angeles, a sprawling, beautiful city with big skies and busy people. I stayed with Deryn, the mother of my American roommate at the Unreasonable Institute. Deryn was an actor, a writer, a director, and a bona fide student of human behavior, as well as a health junkie. She had traveled a great deal and was very interested to meet me, a woman from Pakistan. She gave me my first taste of green tea without sugar. (I found it sharp and bitter, like the medicine my grandmother would make us for stomach pains.) She asked me about village life in Balochistan, questions I answered mostly yes or no. She had framed pictures of her family members smiling and casually doing fun things. In our village, all the children would line up for photos, hold our arms stiff at our sides, and look straight at the camera without blinking, let alone smiling.

Deryn asked me if we exercised in our village. To prove to her that we villagers weren't lazy, I said, "No, we climb mountains. In heels." She was thrilled! She went running every morning, she told me, and asked me to join her.

I was not so thrilled. My rebellion against my family had never included the idea of getting healthy. A woman in my culture running called to mind a lady doing haphazard laps around a garden in *chappals* and a chiffon scarf flowing behind her like a cape. But Deryn would not be denied. She gave me a pair of shoes that I could only think of as boots (since anything that closed around your foot was considered a boot in my village). They had long, fat laces and looked like they should be worn by Olympians. I would later learn that Americans call them sneakers.

The next morning I changed into my least colorful dress. (I realized my multihued dresses made me look like a blob of rainbow in America.) I tied my scarf like a sash and put on the boots. The laces were so long, I had to tie them twice in knots and then shove the ends inside the boot itself. (I had not yet learned the "bunny ears" technique, which to this day I am still mastering.) Just as we were about to leave for the park, Deryn's son called and asked her to babysit his infant son. Saved! I heaved a sigh of relief—until she suggested her neighbor could go running with me instead. I didn't know what to do. She picked up her phone, and suddenly I was stuck again. Not wanting to be impolite, I put my hair in a ponytail and stepped outside in the boots.

The street reminded me of a storybook that Aba had given me once. European men wearing coats laid their hats and overcoats over puddles so that a lady wearing a long gown might step across without getting her feet wet. On either side of the street were impeccably maintained houses, their porches filled with flower pots, and large, tidy sidewalks. I had spent many childhood days wondering what it would be like to look out from the big windows of a tall house, especially the window in the tippy-top room where the roof comes to a point (which I would later learn is called an attic).

I breathed in the delicious clean air of that morning, looked around at the blue sky, and walked up the street that would lead me to the other side of the block and into the park, where I planned to begin my reluctant running, with a stranger no less.

That was when I caught sight of a tall young man waiting at the end of the street. *Uh-oh*, I thought. *Is this the neighbor?* I could still turn around and make an excuse, but this guy was smiling and waiting intently for me. He was very tall, with long, dark hair pulled up smartly, a long, good-looking nose, and dark sunglasses set happily on his face. I was grateful for not being able to see his eyes, as that would have been too awkward.

The idea of being alone with a man outside a professional context was foreign to me. I had had hundreds of official meetings and discussions and phone calls for Sughar, but those were always for a business purpose. Now here I was, in my traditional dress, hair back, big puffy sneakers on my feet, alone with a man for a purely social activity. I didn't know how to act.

"Hi!" I said as brightly as I could. I must have looked like a penguin, but I was there and out of excuses.

After we introduced ourselves—he told me his name was David—I braced myself to run around this beautiful garden where people walked their dogs and mothers pushed babies in carriages. Boys were playing football in the distance. But David had noticed my lack of enthusiasm for running and suggested we walk. He told me he'd heard about me and my work, so we had something to talk about.

David was so kind and curious about Sughar that I found myself opening up to him easily. I told him about the Sughar women in the villages: their laughter, their bright eyes, the way I often felt incapable in the face of their great wisdom. He was so polite and a great listener. He kept asking me more questions, but I caught myself. I wanted to get this walk over with. I didn't want to be intimate with this man whom I had just met.

I asked about his work and was instantly impressed with his vision for the world, his dreams for global peace building and creating effective solutions through technology. He was part of groups in Los Angeles that talked about cultural coexistence and currently worked as a tech analyst for a company working to create alternative energy solutions around the world, but he had previously run a start-up that designed innovative educational software. He had recently moved home from Boston to take care of his mother, who had Stage 4 lung cancer. I felt my heart sink. In Pakistan, a diagnosis of cancer is unfixable, terminal, the end of everything. If someone in your family has cancer, you know that their *qayyamat* (day of judgment) is near, and everyone strives to help the person live fully in the short time remaining. I later learned that his father had died of the same kind of cancer when David was only six years old.

I saw the fear in David's eyes. I told him how important

family is, and we began talking about our siblings, our family lives. I told him about Bili (Cat), the nickname of my youngest sister, and how she was born small and unhealthy but was now growing up quickly and climbing every wall and wardrobe in the house. I told him that all five of my sisters looked up to me, watching and learning. I sometimes feared that it was too much pressure for me and that I would fail as an elder sister.

As I spoke to David about all this, I realized I was sharing my innermost thoughts and feelings—and brought myself back. I was used to sharing those thoughts only with my diary or with my friend Faiza who lived in the neighborhood. I had to leave. As I walked back home, my heart raced—not from exercise but from something else.

"David is a very good person," I later found myself saying to Deryn.

As she looked up at me, the puzzlement on her face slowly turned into an eyebrows-raised expression of mock horror: "Are your uncles going to come and kill him now?"

Two days later I left on a bus for Phoenix, trying to ignore that I was still thinking of David.

CHAPTER 27

Guilt and Reconciliation

I HAD RECEIVED A PHONE CALL FROM VERDE VALLEY School, a small International Baccalaureate boarding school known for its emphasis on global citizenship, located in a place called Sedona, Arizona. I accepted its invitation to speak, as speaking at high schools, colleges, and universities was one of my favorite things to do. I arrived in Phoenix late in the evening and was picked up by some of the school's board members. As they took me to the founder's graceful old Spanish-style home, where I would be staying, they told me about the school and its guiding principles, especially the value of cultural curiosity and service to others. Students came from all over the world to learn, discover one another's cultures, explore nature, and work the red soil together of what I would later discover to be a magical place.

The next morning, my first full day in Sedona, I woke up to beautiful bright light filling the room. I climbed out from beneath the heavy duvet and walked to the window to see where I was—and behold! Pushing aside the thick, flowered curtains, I uncovered a view so exquisite it looked almost unreal: a clear blue sky, a red mountain perfectly framed in the window, dark green patches across the land, and trees near my window. The chilly January landscape reminded me of our mountains at home, and the place felt tinged with something ethereal.

I made my way downstairs to the kitchen, a big room lined with turquoise enamel cabinets, Spanish tile floors with turquoise floor mats, and a dark wooden table at the far end. A window looked out at red rocks. But I stopped in my tracks as I saw David standing there, casually drinking a cup of coffee and talking to my hosts. *What's he doing here? Is he following me?*

David was overjoyed to see me. He had attended the school many years earlier and now sat on the board. As he and I talked, I sipped my water compulsively. The presence of this interesting man was making my heart come out of my chest.

Over the course of three days in Sedona, he and I talked about everything in our hearts and minds. We talked about the presence of God in our lives, the importance of faith, and the importance of a life dedicated to serving others. We didn't have enough time to say all the things we had to say. But when we parted, I decided to stay as far away from him as possible. Even if our hearts and minds matched, our religious and cultural differences were too much. I couldn't bring even more trouble to my family.

———

AFTER SEDONA, MY NEW MENTOR Megan Smith asked me to join her in Vietnam for an event. I had told my heart to stop thinking about David, and by that time it wasn't hard to do. Just before I boarded my flight for Vietnam, my brother Ali called to tell me I'd been selfish. From the day I left for America, my father's health had gone downhill, rapidly. Now Aba was struggling with diabetes and high blood pressure. The guilt sliced my heart to pieces. I hadn't done right by my family. If Aba really was distressed because of me, I had to go fix it.

Five days later I was back in Pakistan. My mother and sisters held me and cried. After everything that had happened the past year, they had been sure they would never see me again. About half an hour later my father came to see me. Silence spread over the house as Fauzia (my middle sister) opened the door for him. A thin figure resembling my father walked in. I burst into tears. *What have I done?* I had given sadness to the man who made me who I was, who stood up for me when nobody else would. When I was asked for in marriage, he had refused; when his friends told him not to send me to expensive schools, he had done it anyway; when I started coloring, he told me I could be an artist; when I started writing, he told me I could be an author. This man had made me into the strong and independent woman I had become. And here he was, extremely saddened and ill. I promised myself that I would do whatever it took to make him happy. Weeping silently, I told him, "I'm back, and I'm not going away."

I had caused enough grief for my family, I decided. In order to make things right, I was going to live the way my father wanted me to, at least on a personal level. If my professional life was hard on him, I would live by my parents' wishes regarding my responsibilities as a daughter. For the next ten months, I poured all my attention into my family. I took the children out, and went to the park with my father every morning to get him moving.

At the same time, I continued planning new projects for Sughar, including the construction of concrete building centers with solar panels for electricity and bathrooms with large windows for good lighting and air. All the Sughar training would take place in these centers, which we decided to call Sughar Hubs. We would invite organizations that dealt with other issues, such as climate change and land rights, to use these centers as meeting spaces as well. This would be in line with Sughar's focus on personal and economic growth in the lives of women. We were thinking bigger now.

During my time in the United States, I had recruited many donors, including TripAdvisor and Women in the World, who generously supported our launch of two Sughar Hubs. We planned new activities, prepared documents that would help us be efficient, listed the names of organizations to pursue, and hired new people. I was so busy with my father and with Sughar that I was able to put Sedona out of my mind.

CHAPTER 28

A Love Marriage in Pakistan

J UST AS I WAS BUSY TRYING TO BE A GOOD DAUGHTER, I met Rehman, who came from a respected family of Sindhi background. He was a branch manager for a life insurance company in Karachi. He was charismatic, well-mannered, and good-looking, someone my father would have chosen for me to marry. And so as he charmed his way into my heart, I began to think a relationship with him made sense.

Rehman and I spoke mostly about our values, our culture, and the need to promote and preserve it. It's often difficult to find men in Pakistan's larger cities who still maintain any love for their tribal heritage. Many fully disconnect themselves, believing that traditional systems are for ignorant men and women. But Rehman loved and respected my work and wanted me to keep moving forward with it. The more I thought about him, the more ideal he looked. We decided to marry as soon as possible so we both could start a life with unified goals.

Things were falling into place—my family was happy with me, Aba and I had resumed our good relationship, and Sughar was more successful every day.

Then one day Amina came back. I was shocked and thrilled to see her alive and happy. I had thought I would never see her beaming face again. It was as if the sun opened our door and walked in, blazing the whole space in radiance and warmth.

"Adi, Adi, Adi," she chanted joyfully, calling me *Sister* and giving me the biggest hug.

Then she asked, "What's happened to you, Adi? Is something stressing you out?"

"No, I'm fine."

"Look at me, Adi," she said. "When I left this office, I took some of your magic with me to face my new life and survive, and I used that magic in the house. I put love, leadership, and power where they belonged. I showed my power and decision making in the house, and soon my husband started respecting me, and the women in the neighborhood started coming to me to receive advice and to seek help. I even started teaching at a nearby school. And now I'm expecting!" Her small eyes got round and big with happiness.

But she wasn't finished. "Adi," she continued, "did I take all of you with me? You look close to accepting defeat."

I was suddenly ashamed. Amina showed me something important that day: that we cannot, in any way, decide what will create another person's happiness. I had worked to unleash potential in women by giving them opportunities and developing their skills as leaders, and like many women activists, I had been forceful in deciding what personal happiness should look like for them, and what their freedom would mean for them. Amina taught me otherwise, and it was a lesson that would serve me well in the next stages of my life and career. I tried to put out of my mind that Amina seemed to think I was not happy.

In July, after four months of our communication, I told Aba about Rehman and asked that he meet him. The day they were to meet, I was excited. *Finally*, I thought, *I will not have to face the many challenges that society throws at unmarried women*. The evening after their meeting, my father came home with a frown and pursed lips. He ate his dinner in silence, telling me he would talk about the meeting the next day.

The next morning, as we strolled along the gravel track in the park where I accompanied him on his walks, he took slow, deep breaths, as the doctors had instructed him.

"Aba, what did you think?" I tried to make my voice sound authoritative and mature, but it came out as a squeak. He took a few more deep breaths, opened his mouth, then closed it again, frowning. I could hear our footsteps as they hit the small pebbles on the track.

"Khali." He tried to sound calm. "I didn't like him."

My father is known to be a great diplomat. People often joked that he could restart a friendship between nations that had been apart for centuries. But in that moment, he showed no signs of diplomacy and got straight to the point. "I just didn't like him."

My heart sank. "Why? What happened?"

"I think," Aba said, looking at his feet as he walked, "I think he will steal your light."

What!? I thought. *Is this you, Aba? You are saying this? You actually believe I have a light?* "What do you mean?" I asked, a little frustrated.

"Khali," he said, "one of the things you've had from when you were a child is blind optimism. Even though this has made me worry about you many times, and I have even disliked it and told you to stop trusting the world, I never, ever wanted it to leave you. This man does not have the slightest optimism. His heart is full of anger, as if the country has taken a big debt from him because of the slight pain he has seen."

Anger flooded my chest, and tears of frustration surfaced in my eyes. My father had often told us that life is a battlefield and everyone is out to get you. He told us that if you are poor, you have to fight to claim what is yours, because it will never be given freely to you. If you are uneducated, you must spend every waking hour learning and face the world as a fighter. And now he disapproved of a man who believed all these same things! How could he tell me all my life that I should not trust men, that I should find a husband who was a respectable Pakistani Muslim from a good family, and then when all these criteria were met, tell me he didn't like him?

But then, as if to save me from this confusion, Aba confessed to something that changed our relationship forever.

CHAPTER 29

Aba's Confession

"I WAS LITTLE WHEN THIS HAPPENED," ABA STARTED. "It was when I first started going to a school, in a village far from ours. I would wake up early in the morning, get ready, and leave as early as four A.M. Many times there were no buses that I could cling to the side of to take me to school. So I often walked for two hours every day, passing a town, a few small villages, and nomadic huts before reaching this place that had become the dearest thing to me. My school. My rope to a better future."

That morning, my father continued, was mild and dewy as he walked to school. He took a shortcut from the main road where the wet dirt sucked at his rubber shoes, which were torn and mended in many places. Sometimes he slipped, and his feet would be covered with yellow and gray dirt.

He slung his stack of books from one shoulder to the other as he walked. He had carefully covered them in old newspapers taped to the inside flaps to keep them fresh for the year, then tied them together with a jute string that he could hold on to and walk more quickly.

The clouds broke, and rays of sun quickly enveloped everything: the mud houses, the neem and babul trees, the tractors standing outside homes, and the kitchen chimneys that were letting out breakfast smoke as the world came alive.

He passed a village full of friendly but conservative people who spoke Sindhi. (My father spoke Brahui as well as Sindhi.) There were no doors on the houses, just the *rilis* hanging in the entranceways for privacy. Cows were being taken out to graze. Other kids too were clutching books to their chests as they walked to the school.

As was often the case, my father's mind was somewhere else, preoccupied with thoughts and dreams. But on that day, he was jarred from his reverie when he saw dust churned up on the dirt road ahead, as if a herd of cattle had just passed through. He quickened his pace, dragging his broken shoe, and saw others hurrying toward a group of people huddled at the side of the road, staring down at something.

When he reached the crowd, with boyish curiosity he pushed people aside so he could see what everyone was looking at. A woman's limp dead body was lying on top of a dead man's bruised and bloodied body. Flies hovered over both of them. My father did not understand. He had not seen death so close before. As harsh as life could be in a village like his, he had not seen blood gushing out of someone's head, soaking their clothes. The same sun rays that he had been admiring a moment earlier, that hugged the trees and made the leaves shine, were now adding to the horror. He slowly pulled himself out of the crowd.

Not comprehending, my father walked slowly away. His arms were unable to hold the books, and his breathing felt tight and forced. When he reached his school, he rinsed off his hair and feet and entered the room. The teacher had not yet arrived. After ten minutes, the teacher was still not there. By this time, the other boys had become restless. They made paper balls and threw them at one another. Some shoved one another and shouted playful dares. Others laughed, sharing jokes. But my father's thoughts couldn't stop churning. He sat on his bench and stared blankly ahead, deaf to the sounds around him.

Forty minutes passed, and there was still no sign of the teacher. The chaos in the classroom intensified. Boys left their seats and walked around the room. My father remained sitting quietly, his face stern and his lips pressed together.

Finally, the teacher rushed in, walked to the blackboard, and wrote down the chapter he would teach that day. The boys took their seats, picked up their books from the floor, and fixed their collars, preparing for the day's studies.

Then the teacher turned around. Blood was splattered all over his shirt.

The terror of the scene my father had witnessed less than an hour before became real to him. The girl murdered on the road was the teacher's niece, and that morning he had killed her, as well as the man who had been lying in the road, in the name of honor. Then he had walked to school to educate boys, as on any normal day at work.

I was shocked when Aba told me this story. I can't remember what I said to him when he finished, but I knew then that despite his opposition to my constant risk taking, he was secretly rooting for me because of the horror he had witnessed. This was why he had moved his family away from his tribe, despite the disapproval and scorn of his own father. This was why he refused to give me away in an exchange marriage before I was born. This was why he never truly stopped me, even though he could have.

I HAD BEEN OFFERED a fellowship at the MIT Media Lab that fall to work with students on creating affordable technology solutions for rural women. (I had been planning to refuse it because I thought I would be planning a wedding.) But after talking with my father that morning, I decided to take it. Rehman was furious.

I went anyway, with new determination. Aba's story empowered and emboldened me to push further whatever the cost.

As soon as I arrived at MIT, the Clinton Global Initiative invited me to speak at its annual meeting in New York, at the generous recommendation of Hillary Clinton.

I was to appear on a panel with Sheryl Sandberg, Christine Lagarde, Bill Clinton, and Bono, whom I had never heard of. That morning while we were waiting in the green room, Rehman contacted me, telling me I was selfish and arrogant, and that he had no time for me or our impending marriage. My head was spinning. His words almost made me vomit. With all that was going on in my life, the worlds I had passed through, and the miles I had traveled, I felt misunderstood and disheartened.

Sheryl, whose confidence and graceful leadership shone through the whole event, sensed my moment of doubt and came over to me.

"This is your stage, Khalida," she told me firmly. "Neither I, nor Christine, nor even that man over there"—she pointed to Bono, who was showing his snakeskin boots to Bill Clinton—"belong on this stage. *You* do. So go get your place."

Her words shook me and reminded me of my purpose. I did exactly as she said, and even though I later asked Bono who he was and what he did for a living, I crushed it!

That October the University of San Diego asked me to give a speech to its students, and afterward I ended up in L.A. for a video shoot. David came to see me. He had kept in touch all these months, sending emails and contributing money to Sughar, even sending me an email after a major earthquake struck Balochistan, asking after me and my family. I never responded, but every time I received a message from him, it was like a stab in the heart of something I could not have.

When I saw him again this time, I realized how different he was from any other man I knew. The way he made me feel my full, powerful self when I was around him; the way he cheered for my successes; and the way he showed immense kindness and empathy for the people I worked to serve—all allowed love to take root in my heart. He was the opposite of Rehman. Marriage to Rehman would have been a marriage of convenience, but nothing in my life could be convenient; my husband wouldn't be either. David and I recognized that the love we saw in each other might be impossible, but we also decided to fight for it.

CHAPTER 30

Borders

THE POWER TO DEFEND OUR LOVE CAME FROM OUR closeness to God. I believe that God gave us several signs that our love was right. The most significant one happened one afternoon at David's mother's house. He had brought flowers to her, as he often did, and while he was arranging them in a vase, one of the buds fell off. It was a tiny, tightly wound bud, the kind that would never bloom even if you put it in water, because it was too young. I picked it up and placed it on my Holy Quran, which is what we do in my culture with peacock feathers, roses, and beautiful leaves. Several days later, as the flowers in the vase were wilting, the bud on the Holy Quran began to bloom. Over the next few days, it continued to unfold, exposing its bright purple heart. And it stayed there, fresh and bold for all to see. We both felt that something higher than us was offering a blessing.

David started a conversation with his mother about our marriage. First wary and now outraged, she thought her son was being blind to the risks that would come with marrying me. "Not only is she a tribal Pakistani girl, but she fights honor killings! I like the person she is, but not where she comes from" was her response.

Meanwhile during a break in my MIT fellowship, I went back to Pakistan. David had written to my father asking for my hand in marriage. My family would surely ask me unending questions about his marriage proposal—and I was not ready to face my father. I worried he would say no. I would have to put up a fight, and I needed to feel grounded before I faced those discussions. So I decided to go to Balochistan first, to check in with my team there and find my solid ground.

At home in the village, I cherished the familiarity of our mud *haveli*, the hugs of my loved ones, the valleys filled with mud homes, and the familiar scent of cow dung burning for chai. Everything was like a soothing balm poured over my restless heart. As exciting as my travels in America had been, the hectic nature of American life struck me as slightly hollow, almost lonely. That night, lying under the mosquito net, I felt as if I'd come back to myself. As the net moved up and down in the light wind, my calm heart whispered to me that it was incomplete. I had left half of it back in bustling Los Angeles.

As the wind blew stronger that night and the sweet scent of the dirt of my homeland teased my senses, I understood for the first time the distance between the land where I had left my heart and the land where I was: thousands of miles of oceans and decisions, of cultures and fates. I wasn't the same person I had been before; love had changed me. I had grown up living indigenously, a village girl in a simple life. But now my fate was intertwined with a man from the other side of the world, a member of that culture we called the West.

THE NEXT MORNING I received a call from the U.S. consulate and was asked to go to Karachi immediately. When I arrived at the consulate the next morning, a man at a window asked for my passport. He picked up a stamp and returned my passport with a canceled visa.

In just a matter of seconds, the doors to being with David were closed for me. The visa officer refused to give me any details—he just asked me to leave his office. I couldn't understand—I had not misused my visa or overstayed it. I was still on my fellowship at MIT. It didn't make sense.

I walked out of the consulate in a daze, got a rickshaw, and only when I reached the door of our small apartment did I allow myself to weep. Then the reality of the situation fully hit me. I was a Pakistani village girl and David was an Italian-American man. The match was impossible, and the world wanted to make sure we knew it. How dare I let my heart wander where it didn't belong? In my naïve and innocent love, I had refused to see the big borders that separated our countries.

I decided that I couldn't lose David because of these borders. He had taught me that I deserved the world. He had taught me to love and to be loved. He had changed my beliefs about marriage. I no longer saw it as the end of a career, but instead as the beginning of a new partnership. I had to strategize. I had to act.

I wrote to the U.S. State Department. I wrote hundreds of emails to activists I'd met all over the world, asking them to help. Soon letters of support poured into the U.S. consulate in Karachi. The most powerful one came from an inspiring woman I had met in the United States, Tina Brown. She had believed in my vision and given me a platform to speak at an event she organized, the Women in the World Summit.

Then the consulate called me again. They gave me back my visa. It had taken over a month, and they never really let me know what had happened in the first place.

My parents had kept quiet during that month, seeing my grief, but they now erupted at me. Aba had told Ammi about the marriage proposal from David, and they were shocked. It seemed my troubles never ended. I was prepared for their outrage, and despite them trying to hide the matter from the children in the house, our conversations grew louder and hurtful. I told Aba that David was the person I truly loved and would spend the rest of my life with. Ammi cried for days, telling me I should give it up: "I've heard [Americans] divorce their wives instantly after marriage. They're not faithful, Khalida!"

Aba sensed my determination, though, and saw that nothing could change my mind. So he cleverly put a big challenge in front of me. "Fine," he said. "If he is Muslim, you marry." He knew he had set the bar impossibly high.

Later that month, when David and I Skyped, he told me he had started to read the English translation of the Holy Quran that I had gifted him, the one with the miraculous bloom. Every time we talked, he asked me questions. As I introduced Islam to David, I felt as if I were reconnecting with my own faith all over again. He told me that he had seen too many signs. God had surprised him too many times and too improbably for it to be considered coincidence. He told me that if being Muslim meant submission to God, then his heart fully submitted.

In Los Angeles a few months later, we found a mosque that would allow David to read the *shahada* (the ritual passage confirming that you witness the oneness of God). According to the religious scholar there, David would remain the person he had been all along but would have more clarity about what God meant to him. He would even keep his name, although lovingly I started calling him Dawood. That day David read the *shahada* in the presence of his mother, his neighbor Deryn, and hundreds of people praying *jumma* (Friday prayers). Loud cheers of God's greatness filled the air. I stood stunned at the presence of God in our lives, at his whole plan.

That evening I was able to tell my parents the good news.

My father was unprepared. "Khali," he said sternly, "be careful. I have been thinking this for some time." He paused. "I really believe David has some connection to the CIA. No one goes around just converting to Islam, especially all these people in the West who have a misconception of our religion."

I was stunned but not shocked. That past December, David's mother had suggested I was part of the Pakistani Inter-Services Intelligence (our equivalent to the CIA). And so the two were now even. It made me believe my father and David's mother had a lot in common: sharp cynicism on the outside and tender hope inside. If only we could get them to meet somewhere, all the doubts would be washed away.

I returned to America to speak at Women in the World, still in limbo about whether I would be able to marry the love of my life.

CHAPTER 31

The Victory of Love

THAT FALL I WAS TO SPEAK AT A CONFERENCE IN VENICE, Italy, organized by Pilosio, an international construction-material manufacturing firm focused on creating sustainable living solutions in developing countries. It would be the perfect place to bring David's and my parents together. I told the conference organizers about the situation; they sponsored the visas and travel for my parents. When my parents applied for the visas, they were refused, but after all kinds of documentation and an incredible amount of time and effort, they finally made their way to Venice. It was my parents' first time traveling in an airplane together, and the first time my mother had had a passport. They arrived at Marco Polo Airport on September 11, 2014, and were interrogated heavily. When I finally saw them nervously walking out of the airport with their suitcase, I realized how far I had brought them from their village life.

In Venice, David and I had strategically canceled the hotel rooms that the conference organizers had booked for us. Instead we booked a small Airbnb flat so the two families could mingle easily. David's mother, Mary Ellen, and her best friend, Carol, a nurse who had helped care for Mary Ellen during her battle with cancer, arrived first. It had been an especially long journey for Mary Ellen, who was going through yet another round of chemotherapy. It had taken much of her hair and relegated her to frequent rests and wheelchairs where they were available.

When I showed up with my parents, we immediately regretted getting such a small apartment. It felt as if everyone was sitting in one another's laps in the tiny living room, and after the formal greetings, a silence overtook the cramped space. My mother got up to make chai in the kitchen. My father, relieved, followed her. I sat next to David's mother, trying to smile, but nothing made the situation better.

That is, until my mother emerged a few moments later carrying a tray of cups filled with golden hot chai. The aroma of cardamom filled the room as the teacups tinkled. As soon as people had chai in their hands, a kind of warmth suffused the room. The tea did its magic. Soon my father made a funny remark, and David's mother responded with a chuckle. My father, encouraged, shared a story in full South Asian style, sitting back on the sofa, his cup of chai in hand. Soon the whole room was relieved, David and I most of all. This moment with the chai (and a few others) would later inspire us to use this magical drink to bring our two vastly different worlds together.

The more our families learned about each other, the closer they became. Their misconceptions melted before our eyes, and soon the borders between their hearts did too. On the third day of the trip, David and I became officially engaged. We had a small celebration with gifts and hugs, while our two very different families bonded.

Back in Pakistan a week later, Aba and Ammi called our relatives to share the news of my engagement to David. Aba did it carefully, making it sound almost as if it were an arranged marriage, and when people asked who the man was, my father responded with "A good Muslim man." That day, as my parents had some of the most difficult conversations of their lives, I felt their love for me anew. I had changed our family dynamic, and my mother and father were handling it with dignity, while bursting with pride for their new son-in-law.

A gathering was arranged in Karachi to officially celebrate my engagement, in the presence of my siblings, cousins, uncles, and aunts. During the celebration, we all danced, and the party went on until midnight. That day I felt like the strongest woman on earth. I was filled with feelings I never thought would live in my heart simultaneously: grief and pride, freedom and submission. I felt braver than ever, knowing that I was marrying a man who stands by me, helps me achieve all that I have dreamed, and reminds me to keep believing in the impossible. I decided I was brave enough to do something I had wanted to do for so many years.

When my uncles, aunts, cousins, siblings, and parents went to sleep, I sat down with Kalsoom. The thick night hummed around us, and as we put henna on each other's hands, I asked her the question that ate at my heart every day. "Kalsoom, where is Sajda?"

She told me her sister had been in Quetta this whole time. Her husband initially took her to his family to receive their blessings, but since they knew the people hunting them down could easily find the boy's family, they left to make a life in Quetta. They lived every day in fear of being found.

Relief and pain washed over me at once. It seemed a hard life for Sajda—she was away from her siblings, her home, and her family, but she was alive. Kalsoom told me they would sometimes meet in far-off places, and Sajda would appear in a black veil. My heart skipped to my throat, imagining sweet Sajda, that thin little girl who laughed so much and wanted so much out of life, wearing a burqa, afraid for her life every day. I asked Kalsoom to call her, and after four long years, I heard the tiny voice of my cousin. I promised I would bring her back to the family. I didn't know how, but I would.

CHAPTER 32

God's Justice

WITHIN A FEW WEEKS, DAVID CALLED TO LET ME know that my soon-to-be mother-in-law was in critical condition. In my culture, having a mother-in-law is a sign of good fortune; when a girl leaves her home, a new mother awaits her in the new home. I wasn't one of those fortunate ones. Way before I could learn to cook her special dishes or go shopping with her, my mother-in-law was leaving me. I spent months at her bedside, praying or telling her stories of my village, and when the sadness broke David's and my heart, I would play Bollywood songs and dance for her.

In November 2014, two months before our wedding in Karachi, David's mother left us. She was buried next to her husband, Louis, David's father, which was her wish. That day, at the graveyard, I knew David was burying his childhood. It wasn't just a chapter of his life that had closed but a whole volume. We were both devastated, but we knew the only way to heal was to strengthen our bond.

That week I flew to Pakistan. As per my mother-in-law's wish, we kept the date we had set before her health worsened. I had a month left to plan a five-hundred-person wedding. But once I landed in Pakistan, more shocking news awaited me: Uncle Liaqat had been diagnosed with Stage 4 stomach cancer. His body had gone into paralysis, and he hardly spoke or ate anything.

Would the shocking incidents of my life never end? I could not imagine my fierce uncle facing such pain and illness. In spite of the trauma he had caused my family, I decided to visit him and pray for him. Since he had been living in Karachi, I had seen a change in him. I had seen him talk to Kalsoom and her siblings with love. I had seen him bring groceries to them, and when I visited, he would sit and talk with me about my work, asking me questions.

I didn't know where or when the boundaries of hate had ended and love had started in my heart. But I did remember learning to forgive after a meal with Kalsoom's mother.

About a year after Khadija's murder, people were doing a good job of making it look like she had never existed. But Khadija spoke through the walls of that house, through the wind that passed beneath the neem tree in the center of the house, as if a witness to the loss.

Ammi had gone to visit neighbors, and Khadija's mother and I had this time to ourselves. My aunt and I sat on the floor of her kitchen, made from loose bricks, bamboo, and straw. We shared a meal in silence. Some kids played out in the yard. All I wanted was to look into her eyes and understand: how was she living her life with such a loss?

But her eyes were content. I had often seen her cry when she washed clothes or made a fire for a meal, but I never thought I would see this peace in her eyes. I instantly knew that she had forgiven Liaqat. Not forgotten, but forgiven the people who took her daughter from her, murdered her, and erased her from the face of the earth. I learned the biggest lesson about forgiveness that day, that when you forgive, you don't do it for others but to relieve yourself. You do it to allow yourself to be unburdened, so that you are present for those who are around you. She had chosen to forgive my uncle so she could serve and be with those in her family who still lived.

It took me a long time, but I slowly learned to forgive, not just my uncle but every single person I had a grudge against. It allowed me to become stronger, freer, and more able to do the work I wanted to do.

So that day, as I walked toward the little Karachi apartment where Kalsoom and her siblings lived, I kept reminding myself that I had forgiven my uncle. What I saw that day, I would not forget for the rest of my life.

The tiny, humble apartment had two plastic floor mats, a small fridge, and heaps of books as its only contents. In the center, my uncle lay on the floor, his head in Kalsoom's lap as she stroked his hair and fed him soup. The person who had taken my cousin Sajda's childhood from her, who had taken the life of my cousin Khadija, who had deprived the others of their parents, who had taught that family to live in fear, had in the end learned many things from these children. The biggest was that he had learned to love. He had learned to bring coloring books for the little ones, to listen to Kalsoom and bring the exact groceries she asked him to, and to wipe tears from the children's faces when they were scared. He had learned to tell them stories at night that made them laugh and took their pain away, even if just for a little bit. He had learned to have a family. And right when he did, God was taking it away from him. His life was leaving him, and at that moment my eyes couldn't help but weep for him.

As I took off my shoes at the door, the sound of my sandals broke the silence, and my weakened uncle exclaimed, "Look! Khajo is here!" (Khadija's nickname). Everyone's face drained, because they all saw that he was looking past me and seeing someone else standing there, looking at him. That day I knew that all these years, Khadija had lived right here, next to me, waiting for the moment when my uncle recognized her presence. I felt ashamed for not having seen her, for not having made her be seen. And that day I promised to write this book, to give testimony to her murder, to tell her truth to the world.

Just two months later, in February 2015, barely a month after my wedding to the man with whom I had fallen in love, Liaqat passed away.

We have a saying in my tribe—in God's justice there is delay, but no darkness.

CHAPTER 33

A Big Tribal Wedding

ALL THIS MIGHT NEVER HAVE HAPPENED. DESPITE being a woman, I have freedom, education, and authority. Some days I wonder if it all could be a beautiful illusion. It was so unlikely that my life would be so different from the lives of my cousins and the other girls in my village, yet there I was, sitting next to a man from the other side of the world, celebrating our union with my tribe. *Can this be real?*

These were my thoughts on the day of my wedding to David, as we sat together on the stage in the wedding hall in Karachi, decorated like a king's palace, with chandeliers and curtains of roses and marigolds, everything so glamorous. The wedding celebration lasted ten days and included more than five hundred guests at different points. From all across the country my tribal relatives filled buses and vehicles to come and be part of this unique wedding.

On the day of the main ceremony, I dressed in my beautiful red *lehenga* (skirt) with intricate gold embellishment, chosen a month earlier at a local wedding dress market. My gold jewelry was draped over me like fruit on a full, ripe tree: a necklace, earrings, and my favorite large round nose ring with a beaded gold string attached to an earring, a set that David and his mother had given me as a wedding gift.

On my wedding day, no matter how hard I tried, my tears wouldn't stop. They soaked the makeup that five patient women had applied in an expensive parlor earlier that day. I cried for so many reasons: for the heavy guilt I felt in my heart; for the sadness I felt for my cousins who were dancing to the traditional drumbeat, holding their little ones, waving at me frequently, joyful that I was marrying the love of my life and a man of my choice, but knowing they might not have a similar option; and for my gratitude at being so blessed.

As I looked out from behind my net veil dusted with gold stars, I saw the faces of girls who had kept me up at night. I saw my childhood friends who now had children of their own. Memories poured through me: laughter, tuneless songs, hair flying through the air, running after a herd of cows, bare feet churning up dirt, dancing in the July rains in Khuzdar, telling stories under a sky coated with stars. I was awash in other memories that were not as happy: pushing my face into a pillow so I could cry, feeling so helpless when a friend was married at eleven, the confusion of it all. My lives and their lives were the same, my face and theirs were the same, but my fate had taken a different turn. One small thing had made the difference: education.

Education had given me freedom, confidence, and an

understanding of my rights. Education was the thin line that separated me from those who danced before me now, celebrating my wedding, which was also a celebration of freedom—my freedom to choose. Gratitude and sadness filled my heart in equal measure. The man I chose to marry, with whom I had fallen in love, was very different from me and my world.

My sisters Fatima and Fauzia watched me from the far side of the hall, their heavily lined eyes shining with pride. The lights felt suddenly brighter, and the music louder, people's voices echoing in my ears as tears ran down my face. The drumbeat went on. My sweaty and happy father circulated and received congratulations from everyone. My mother beamed, my sisters looked glamorous as they hosted our guests, so many of whom were shepherds and tradesmen. Many had never been to a city.

The magic of this evening also made me think, *What if, all those years ago, my father had agreed to give me away before I was born in order to bring his brother a wife?*

As I looked out over the crowd, I imagined the person I might have become. She had been married off as soon as she bled, to a tribe she knew nothing about. I saw her washing dishes and cleaning the house. I saw her cooking with other wives and serving the men first. I saw her waiting shyly in a corner until they were finished, then taking the leftovers into the kitchen, huddling over them, and eating with the other women. Perhaps they would gossip, laugh a little, or whisper something funny; perhaps she would laugh too, her giggle reaching out of the kitchen, and she would catch herself and remember to be quiet.

This imaginary woman crept into my heart and lodged there, next to my great joy at marrying my chosen man. The opportunities given to me had made me all that I had become, and they would continue to shape my path. I had a father who believed in me, cherished me, and had fulfilled his fatherly duties by educating me. And most important, when the time came, he had told me about honor and what it meant to him, which was what it had come to mean to me.

In the distance, among shimmering dresses and happy faces, Kalsoom never stopped dancing to the drumbeats. Her joy was about something bigger than this wedding, something that perhaps only I could understand. Her whole being seemed to say that this day when I married the love of my life was the day love *did* win in our family. Her sister *did* win.

CHAPTER 34

Gang of Thieves

MANY MOONS AGO, IN A VALLEY BETWEEN THE LARGE mountains and cold waterfalls of Balochistan, a man traveled to Sindh and found himself in love with a woman in a tiny village with open skies and vast green fields. In those times, love between a man and a woman not arranged to each other was unheard of, unspoken. The man belonged to a different tribe, so marriage to this woman—who refused to leave his thoughts as he awoke in the mornings and slept at night—was impossible.

All he could do was visit the village for one reason or another and hope to glimpse her beauty as she laughed with her friends or walked with grace and joy carrying water pots on her head. He was secretive about his trips to her neighborhood, but Fatima, clever and in her twenties, sometimes noticed this young man standing behind a tree or sitting near the water canal watching her as she washed clothes with her friends. She would look up, see him, and

quickly avert her gaze. She knew very well that if her brothers, her uncles, or her father caught her, they would dig out
her eyes for staring at a strange man.

Then one day, using only the language of his eyes, Allah
Ditta asked Fatima to come meet him behind the fields.
The next day she couldn't resist.

During that first meeting, their hearts decided they
couldn't live without each other. They must marry. But discussion of such a topic was impossible for both their tribes.
So they decided to elope, leaving behind their worlds and
creating a new one of their own. One dark night, Fatima
gathered a few of her belongings, made a traveling heap of
them, and ran off with Allah Ditta to marry him in a distant village mosque.

The news spread like fire devouring a forest. Before the
young couple could leave the village limits, it reached the
ears of the elders. They were caught.

The matter was taken immediately to the village tribal
leader. He saved Fatima from being murdered by her family in the name of honor but kept her in his large palace
until a decision could be made about what to do with her.
Allah Ditta, outmatched and in danger, was told to leave
and never return. So he left.

But during the night he traveled to the palace of the
tribal leader. There he charmed a guard, using his good-
natured ways, to sneak a message to Fatima.

After hours of waiting behind the large walls of the palace, Allah Ditta saw the sorrowful eyes of Fatima emerge
between the cracks. He sent a rope over the wall, and she

tied it around her waist. Allah Ditta pulled it with all his strength until Fatima was on the other side. They quietly and joyously reunited, and without a word they fled into the dark, toward a village where Allah Ditta had organized a small wedding ceremony for them, and then to the mountains.

Every day they traveled by foot, crossing one village, then another, one district after another. Before long Fatima was pregnant. With the baby in her belly, she was often hungry but had nothing to eat or drink. So when Allah Ditta didn't return quickly from trying to find a safe place to stay, she would dress like a man and walk into the markets. She would buy herself food and sneak back home.

Then the child was born. It was a gorgeous baby boy with big eyes whom they lovingly called Liaqat, a name given to those who were strong and able. They wanted to raise him to be a strong young man who never had to run from anyone.

But fate had different plans for them. Fatima's family found her. In her fear and distress, but before running from her little hut, she handed her baby to a gang of thieves whom they had befriended on their travels. Fatima was caught. She was beaten and kept away from Allah Ditta, who spent months looking for her. Even after finding her, he could not steal her back.

As the years passed, the baby boy grew fond of the thieves and their rugged lifestyle. Even after Allah Ditta triumphed at a big fight and brought Fatima home, the child remained with the group. He visited his parents only sometimes and finally moved into their home in his adolescence. The family, having never lost hope or love for one another, finally lived in contentment, without fear, and had several more children. My uncle Liaqat, the eldest, was the strongest of them all.

Epilogue

As I write this, it's been three years since David and I became lifelong partners. I am the happiest and strongest I have ever been. David has given me immense love, made me feel powerful and fearless. Shortly after our marriage in 2015, he left his job to embark on this journey with me, to help me work to unleash potential in tribal women in Pakistan. With his support and the guidance of an amazing board of directors, we have registered the Sughar Foundation as a 501(c)(3) nonprofit in the United States. By so doing, we are now able to fully scale our work and replicate the Sughar Centers all across Pakistan.

After our wedding in Karachi, David and I planned another celebration on the gorgeous campus of Verde Valley School in Sedona, Arizona. We wanted to share the story of our miraculous union with everyone we loved who could not attend the wedding in Karachi. But after experiencing the many hardships of bringing our two families together,

we realized how much fear and misunderstanding live between our two very different worlds, and how few are the
opportunities to connect people across borders. Instead of
spending the money on celebrating the two of us for one
day, we decided to use it to launch a social enterprise to
build bridges across our two cultures, giving 50 percent of
its profits for much-needed projects to support women and
children in Pakistan. So we canceled the celebration and
launched our new initiative, The Chai Spot.

The Chai Spot was an overnight success! People came
to Sedona from all over the world and loved and celebrated
the vision behind the place—the delicious chai, the bright
decorations, and ambiance borrowed from my country.
And just like that, it became a place where people came to
share and receive love, talk about peace, and learn about
the beautiful aspects of Pakistani culture that are neglected
by the media and remain unknown (and therefore scary) to
most Americans.

Then, after the trauma of the 2016 elections in the
United States increased misunderstandings among people
and sent a new wave of fear through the hearts of American citizens, David and I worked to start another initiative
that took our peace-building efforts to the next level: Otaq,
a boutique Pakistani guesthouse experience. We had
learned that hospitality is an effective way to build bridges,
and what better way than to invite people to stay in our *otaq*
decorated the traditional Pakistani way, with plush rugs, in-
tricately embroidered fabrics, and exotic floor seating? We
provide our guests with a glimpse into the rich and diverse

culture of Pakistan: they can visit Pakistan right here in America and experience a sliver of what David and I love most about my country.

These three busy years have been the crux of my journey, changing me in ways I never imagined. Writing this book has taken me on a self-transformational journey. I have grown in new ways and am reminded of the beautiful stories and customs that make me who I am. David and I have taken each other to our worlds, introducing each to the other's life, and become accustomed to each other's realities.

I took David to my tribe around Sindh, introduced him to cousins who showed him how to play cricket, aunts who taught him how to speak Brahui, and uncles who shared stories and chai with him. I took him to a Sughar village where we were greeted with such joy and love that they threw us an impromptu wedding celebration. We arrived unannounced in the morning, and by afternoon local musicians were drumming and singing, while the entire village danced in our honor and presented us with gifts. Afterward they served us chai, biscuits, and laughter. This tiny village, where the people struggle daily, felt such gratitude and enrichment from our work. The women teased me and laughed with me, while the men welcomed David in ways that transcended language.

David, for his part, took me to his family in Chicago and introduced me to his cousins, who welcomed me with love and open arms and showed me all around their city.

In these years, the further my life has traveled from my tribal origins, the more it has brought me back to its values and how those values, if used properly, can enable women to thrive in our traditional society. Despite my anger at the destructive customs in my culture, I appreciate the overwhelming beauty of everything else. After crossing many continents, social classes, and cultures, I see clearly what a blessing we have in the wholeness, groundedness, and intuitiveness of our tribal wisdom—and, most of all, our core belief in nurturing honor.

I have come to see that the presence of honor, of dignity, in our lives is the strength that enables us to thrive. It will help us reevaluate our cultural shortcomings in raising the status of women. I have come to know that the problem is not honor and tribal communities' sheer need to preserve it. It is the way they do it that is wrong. Despite the fact that women are a tremendous and indispensable part of the society, and that women's status is recognized, celebrated, and protected in Islam, they are demoralized in traditional cultures and households. The mothers who give birth to the sons later get disrespected *by* those sons. The wives who dedicate their lives to their husbands get beaten and abused. The daughters who cherish their fathers are given in marriage without their consent. Sisters, mothers, wives, and daughters are being killed because they demanded their right to freedom and right to love. There is absolutely no honor in any of these acts, and that is not the kind of honor my country aspires to.

In my fight against honor killings, I have woven honor into my dialogues by drawing the attention of tribal leaders to what true honor *should be* for them. I have made it my goal to do what my father did for me when he sat me down many years ago and told me how I would honor him. I have made it my mission to redefine honor, to bring it back to where it belongs. Honor is not the inheritance of men. Every woman should have honor.

You should have honor.

I should have honor.

Acknowledgments

I AM EXTREMELY GRATEFUL TO ALLAH FOR GIVING ME the power to tell my story. As I learned in the past two years, it's an uncomfortable process that makes you fully vulnerable. I am grateful to my husband, David (Dawood), for helping me with each part of the book, as well as for coping with my moods, sadnesses, anxieties, and at times cravings for rare foods. I am grateful to my father, who helped edit the book, and to my mother, Noor Jehan, for writing stories of her childhood, helping me with all the hardest details, and holding me when I cried.

I am grateful to my brothers, Ali and Sajjad, who are my heart's joy, for helping me to find and select images; to my sister Fatima for sharing childhood stories with Fauzia and me; and to Sabeena and Safia for keeping me fed during the whole crazy time. I am grateful to my little siblings for giving me joy and keeping me amused through depressing times. I am so very grateful to Kalsoom for being strong and taking charge, and to her siblings for working hard in the face of adversity and going to the best universities in Karachi. I am so very grateful to my editor, Andrea Walker, for her patience, understanding, and love throughout this process, for listening to me, for putting up with my sorrows, and for being there with an open heart guiding me to move forward. I am grateful to my agents, Margaret Riley King and Jennifer Walsh, who have supported me, lifted me up, and guided me during this whole process. I am grateful to Emily Black, who helped me string together the huge bulk of my stories.

I am deeply grateful for the love and support of my mentor and friend Sheryl Sandberg, without whom this book would not be possible. I am immensely grateful to Megan Smith, my dear friend and mentor, who helped me in the most desperate times, guiding me with love and connecting me with the whole world. I am so thankful to my sister Ruma Bose, for being there for me, holding my hand, and supporting me, and to Neha Sangwan, my dear friend, who many times during these years housed me and kept me fed. I am grateful to the board members of the Sughar Foundation, Janelle Gale, Lila Igram, and Abigail Disney, for believing in me and for being kind and gentle with me. I am grateful to my advisers and supporters Zehra Ali, Daniel Epstein, Ethan Zuckerman, and Joi Ito. Thank you for believing in me and my vision. Thank you for standing strong with me when I wasn't my strongest self.

I am thankful to Sharmeen Obaid-Chinoy, Saba Gul, Moira Forbes, Tina Brown, Zainab Salbi, Shannon Grewer, Eyal Aronoff, Chris Anderson, Kalsoom Lakhani, Amy Griffin, Juliet de Baubigny, Lisa Ferri, Sarah Hall, Sarah

Baker, and Joanne Moore for providing your love and support in so many ways . . . it has been that support and unwavering belief in me that led to this book and to all that will come.

I am grateful to the Aurat Foundation and the Takhleeq Foundation in Pakistan for their work, and to the late Sabeen Mahmud and Asma Jahangir for their hard work and for shattering the glass ceiling, which made it easier for those of us who came after them. I am grateful to Northwestern University for bringing my mother to America. It had the unintended consequence of helping me a lot with the book. I am grateful to Wendy Lippman of Tlaquepaque for taking a chance on The Chai Spot and our unique business model. And finally I am grateful to all those friends, families of friends, flightmates, seatmates, and complete strangers who came up to me in the past decade of my journey to help, to say a word of kindness or encouragement, and to those who hosted me in their homes and gave me food, water, support, and their sheer belief.

I love you all so very much.

Glossary

- *aba*—father
- *adi*—sister
- *Ali*—name of author's eldest brother
- *Allah Ditta*—name of author's paternal grandfather
- *ama*—mother
- *ammi*—mother (Urdu)
- *appa*—elder sister
- *badli*—exchange
- *baligh*—mature
- *bhalla aba*—elder father; grandfather
- *bhalla ama*—elder mother; grandmother
- *bishenk*—a wool fabric to roll the dough for breadmaking
- *Bismillah*—Begin in the name of Allah
- *Brahui*—Mountain Dweller, indigenous tribe and language of the author
- *burqa*—long black veil

- *chador*—big scarf worn as a veil
- *chai*—tea
- *cham cham*—pattycake
- *chappals*—sandals
- *charpoy*—wooden jute cot
- *chole*—spicy chickpeas
- *dakh rakh*—the traditional healing method of enclosing patient for forty days
- *diyat*—compensation
- *dupatta*—headscarf
- *Eid*—Muslim festival after thirty days of Ramadan
- *Fatima*—name of author's younger sister
- *Fatima*—name of author's paternal grandmother
- *Fauzia*—name of author's middle sister
- *fitu*—hopscotch
- *ghee*—oil
- *gulab jamun*—a dessert consisting of round chickpea flour balls dipped in rose water and sugar syrup
- *haveli*—house with a large yard and courtyard
- *Hudud Ordinances*—laws in Pakistan that were enacted in 1977 as part of then–military ruler Zia-ul-Haq's "Sharization" or "Islamization" process
- *Jattak*—name of a Brahui clan in Balochistan
- *jugar*—making things work with creative problem solving
- *jumma*—Friday prayers
- *kaka*—uncle
- *Kalsoom*—name of author's cousin
- *kari*—a woman to be murdered; literally, "black"

- *Khadija*—name of author's cousin; Kalsoom's sister
- *khat*—wooden jute bed
- *kho*—hide-and-seek
- *lehenga*—long Pakistani skirt
- *Liaqat*—name of author's uncle
- *Manzoor*—name of author's uncle
- *Masha Allah*—praise to God
- *mate*—white clay eaten by pregnant women
- *Mengal*—name of a clan in Balochistan
- *mistai*—good news
- *Mohim Khan*—name of author's maternal grandfather
- *mullah*—religious teacher
- *nikai*—ceremonial signing of the wedding contract
- *Noor Jehan*—name of author's mother
- *otaq*—room where guests are entertained
- *paratha*—flatbread fried in oil
- *pati*—chest for clothes
- *P.B.U.H.*— peace be upon him
- *phidi*—betrothal of a daughter in marriage before her birth; literally, "from the belly"
- *qayyamat*—day of judgment
- *qisas*—retaliation
- *rehmat*—blessing
- *rili*—traditional quilt
- *roti*—flatbread baked over an open fire
- *sabr*—patience
- *Sajjad*—name of author's younger brother
- *shahada*—ritual to declare the oneness of God

- *shalwar qameez*—long shirt worn over large pants, the traditional outfit for both women and men
- *Sharam Naz*—name of author's maternal grandmother
- *shonki*—someone who wants too many things
- *Sikander*—name of author's father
- *Sufi*—a sect of Islam
- *sughar*—skilled and confident
- *sulaimani chai*—a water-based black tea with spices
- *talib*—a student
- *taliban*—a group of students
- *waro*—dairy farm
- *wata sata*—exchange marriages
- *zal mazur*—servant of the wife
- *zina*—extramarital sex

About the Author

KHALIDA BROHI is an award-winning activist and entrepreneur. Her nonprofit, Sughar, unleashes leadership skills and economic power in tribal women in Pakistan. Brohi has been named one of *Newsweek*'s "25 Under-25 Young Women to Watch" and *Forbes*'s "30 Under 30" for social entrepreneurship, and she was a Director's Fellow at the MIT Media Lab. She has received the Coretta Scott King A.N.G.E.L. Award from the King Center and the inaugural Buffett Award for Emerging Global Leaders from Northwestern University. Brohi has addressed numerous global forums, such as TEDGlobal, the Clinton Global Initiative, Women in the World, Davos, the World Affairs Council, Google's Zeitgeist, and Facebook's Women's Leadership Day. In 2015, Brohi and her husband, David, co-founded The Chai Spot and later Otaq LLC, which promote the beautiful aspects of Brohi's cultural heritage while uplifting women and children in Pakistan in order to create healthy lives and eradicate damaging customs. She has served on the board of directors of the International Youth Foundation and is currently executive director of the Sughar Foundation. She and her husband split their time between the United States and Pakistan.

khalidabrohi.com
Facebook.com/kbpakistan
Twitter: @KhalidaBrohi
Instagram: @khalida.brohi

About the Type

This book was set in Baskerville, a typeface designed by
John Baskerville (1706–75), an amateur printer and typefounder,
and cut for him by John Handy in 1750. The type became
popular again when the Lanston Monotype Corporation
of London revived the classic roman face in 1923.
The Mergenthaler Linotype Company in England and the
United States cut a version of Baskerville in 1931, making it
one of the most widely used typefaces today.